Essential Skills for the Peer Recovery Workforce

JORDAN PEER RECOVERY TRAINING

Promoting the Journey towards Recovery through
Culturally Responsive Peer Support

Essential Skills for the Peer Recovery Workforce
Jordan Peer Recovery Training
Second Edition

Dr. Masica Jordan, LLC

Liability Disclaimer

You assume all risk associated with the facilitation and use of this training and/or textbook and all Dr. MJ, LLC products and services. Furthermore, such use of products does not constitute a therapeutic relationship with Dr. MJ, LLC, any of its authors, trainers or with anyone associated with development or delivery of services. All training is designed to assist you with facilitating discussions and training.

We have made every effort to ensure that information is correct and helpful, Dr. Masica Jordan, LLC, Dr. Masica Jordan, the author (s), publisher (s) and associate members, board members, officers, affiliates and advisors do not assume and hereby disclaim any liability to any party for any harm alleged to be the result of the facilitation and use of all Dr. MJ, LLC services.

The process of exploring might open up levels of awareness and provoke realizations that cause uncomfortable feelings, sadness, guilt, anxiety, anger, pain, frustration, loneliness, and/or helplessness. Individuals may need to seek professional help immediately if they experience thoughts of suicide or homicide, uncontrollable crying, decrease in day-to-day activities, overwhelming sadness, overwhelming guilt and/or shame, loss of enjoyment in activities over a period of seven days, isolation, extended sleep patterns over a period of seven days, anger and/or hostility. In some cases, during the process of change major life decisions are made, in others, traumatic events are reflected upon. This process of growth and self-actualization can cause significant impacts to lifestyles and relationships. The process of helping, identification and prevention is not an exact science; we make no guarantees or warranties regarding outcomes. By agreeing to provide and/or participate in training, you agree to these terms discussed and release the founder, author, her Board, affiliates, and the publisher of liability in all matters pertaining to the use of any resource or material.

I also agree to the following terms and conditions:

AGREEMENT TO FOLLOW TRAINING POLICIES. I agree to abide by all Dr. MJ, LLC documented training guidelines and procedures.

ASSUMPTION OF THE RISKS AND RELEASE. I recognize that there are certain inherent risks associated with the above described activity and I assume full responsibility for personal injury to myself and my organization, and further release and discharge Dr. Masica Jordan, LLC for injury, loss or damage arising out of my or my organization's use of or presence during a training of Dr. Masica Jordan, LLC, whether caused by the fault of myself, my organization, Dr. Masica Jordan, LLC or other third parties.

INDEMNIFICATION. I agree to indemnify and defend Dr. Masica Jordan, LLC, Dr. Masica Jordan, the author (s), publisher (s) associate members, board members, officers, affiliates, advisors and associates against all claims, causes of action, damages, judgments, costs or expenses, including attorney fees and other litigation costs, which may in any way arise from my or my organization's use of services or presence during an event of Dr. Masica Jordan, LLC.

APPLICABLE LAW. Any legal or equitable claim that may arise from participation in the above shall be resolved under Maryland law.

NO DURESS. I agree and acknowledge that I am under no pressure or duress to continue in this training or to use this textbook or any other product, and by continuing I have made this Agreement under no duress and I have been given a reasonable opportunity to review it before continuing in the training or use of the textbook or product. I further agree and acknowledge that I am free to have my own legal counsel review this Agreement if I so desire.

ARM'S LENGTH AGREEMENT. This Agreement and each of its terms are the product of an arm's length negotiation between the Parties. In the event any ambiguity is found to exist in the interpretation of this Agreement, or any of its provisions, the Parties, and each of them, explicitly reject the application of any legal or equitable rule of interpretation which would lead to a construction either "for" or "against" a particular party based upon their status as the drafter of a specific term, language, or provision giving rise to such ambiguity.

ENFORCEABILITY. The invalidity or unenforceability of any provision of this Agreement, whether standing alone or as applied to a particular occurrence or circumstance, shall not affect the validity or enforceability of any other provision of this Agreement or of any other applications of such provision, as the case may be, and such invalid or unenforceable provision shall be deemed not to be a part of this Agreement.

DISPUTE RESOLUTION. The parties will attempt to resolve any dispute arising out of or relating to this Agreement through friendly negotiations amongst the parties. If the matter is not resolved by negotiation, the parties will resolve the dispute using the below Alternative Dispute Resolution (ADR) procedure.

Any controversies or disputes arising out of or relating to this Agreement will be submitted to mediation in accordance with any statutory rules of mediation. If mediation is not successful in resolving the entire dispute or is unavailable, any outstanding issues will be submitted to final and binding arbitration under the rules of the American Arbitration Association. The arbitrator's award will be final, and judgment may be entered upon it by any court having proper jurisdiction.

I HAVE READ THIS DOCUMENT AND UNDERSTAND IT. I FURTHER UNDERSTAND THAT BY JOING THIS TRAINING AND/OR USING THIS TEXTBOOK, I VOLUNTARILY SURRENDER CERTAIN LEGAL RIGHTS

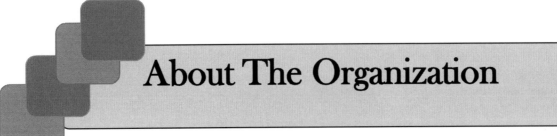

About The Organization

Jordan Peer Recovery
Dr. Masica Jordan, LLC

About Us

Jordan Peer Recovery, *a division of Dr. Masica Jordan, LLC (Dr. MJ, LLC)* is a training institution offering innovative solutions like; a proprietary peer recovery workforce assessment, State and National Board (NAADAC) approved peer recovery trainings, specialized trainings, a peer recovery workforce registry and many other services to support the peer recovery workforce.
Dr. Masica Jordan, LLC is the leading entity for building cultural responsiveness within the peer recovery workforce.

Peer-Led Organization
We are a peer-led organization. Every member is a part of the Peer Recovery Workforce. Dr. Jordan started the organization because of her own recovery journey and after losing multiple loved ones, including her father to substance use disorder. Dr. Jordan is inspired to create a better present and future for those in recovery and to ensure no one is left behind.

Aptitude
We believe in our peer recovery workforce and are driven to support their growth by building aptitude to establish a talented peer recovery workforce that cannot just "win the war on drugs," but demolish it. This is our passion and to do so we have created a full portfolio of assessments, trainings and other resources. Our training is offered in all 50 states as a NAADAC-approved training, as well as a State-Board approved training program. Peers who complete training through Jordan Peer Recovery Training are eligible for both National and State certifications. We utilize in-person, online and hybrid training methods and offer specialized trainings, in addition to our 60-hour core curriculum.

Culturally Responsive
Cultural responsiveness refers to the use and delivery of culturally responsive recovery resources. The Substance Abuse and Mental Health Services Administration (SAMHSA) defines cultural responsiveness as the ability to interact effectively with people of different cultures. In practice, both individuals and organizations can be culturally responsive. Culture must be considered at every step of the Strategic Prevention Framework (SPF). "Culture" is a term that goes beyond just race or ethnicity. It can also refer to such characteristics as age, gender, sexual orientation, disability, religion, income level, education, geographical location, or profession. Cultural responsiveness means to be respectful and responsive to the health beliefs and practices—and cultural and linguistic needs—of diverse population groups. Developing cultural responsiveness is also an evolving, dynamic process that takes time and occurs along a continuum.

For more information and additional resources visit **www.JordanPeerRecovery.com**

Introduction to Essential Skills for the Peer Recovery Workforce

Peer Recovery Specialists are role models of recovery values and principles, choosing to help others with struggles and issues that the worker knows and understands. Peer Recovery Specialists accomplish this by helping to identify and remove barriers, as well as triggers, for treatment for individuals receiving services from inpatient or outpatient programs. Peer Recovery Specialists must demonstrate their ability to provide effective services, which include advocacy, mentoring, education, recovery support, and engaging in ethical responsibility. Beyond the application of core competencies, Peer Recovery Specialists must master essential skills in order to acquire and maintain employment as peers.

Essential skills are a combination of techniques involving people, social situations, communication, character, attitude, career attributes, and social and emotional intelligence quotients. This is among other factors that also enable those to navigate their environment, work well with others, perform accordingly, and achieve their goals with complementing hard skills.

Nearly every task of a peer recovery specialist, and other employment options, utilize essential skills. These include, but are not limited to, community-based services, non-profits, and healthcare. The tactics provide the foundation for learning additional on-the-job skills, plus they enable the peer recovery workforce to promote their careers and acclimate to workplace changes.

Besides common essential skills, there are additional habits that peers must develop that are specific to peer recovery. This course is designed to promote the development of common, as well as, peer-recovery-focused essential skills.

Learning Objectives

Section 1 – Universal Essential Skills
- [ ] Interview 101
  - Preparing for the Interview
  - Responsible Preparation and What to Wear
  - You: Sharing your Story
  - What is a Career Portfolio?
  - Interview Responses
  - The Elevator Pitch
  - Common Peer Recovery Interview Questions
  - Interview Tips
  - Presenting Your Weakness as a Strength
  - Practicing for the Interview
  - Accepting the Offer
  - Recovery Safe Celebration
  - Supportive Transition
  - Professional Etiquette
  - Computer Literacy

Section 2 – Professional Communication
  - Workplace and Professional Etiquette
  - Dos and Don'ts
  - SOLER
  - Listening and Understanding
  - Empathetic Communication
  - Sharing Information
  - Practice Effective Communication
  - Writing to the Needs of the Audience
  - Reading Independently
  - Being Assertive
  - Writing Clinical SOAP Notes

Section 3 – Working on a Team
  - Working Across Different Ages, Irrespective of Gender, Race, Religion or Political Persuasion
  - Applying Teamwork to a Range of Situations, e.g. Future Planning and Crisis Problem-Solving
  - Working Within the Role Boundary of a Peer Recovery Workforce
  - Knowing How to Define a Peer Recovery Role as Part of the Treatment Team
  - Understanding the Roles of Different Treatment Team Members

- o Working as an Individual and as a Member of a Team
- o Identifying the Strengths of Treatment Team Members
- o Coaching and Mentoring Skills, Including Giving Feedback to Peers, Treatment Team Members and Other Providers

Section 4 – Problem Solving
- o Empowering the Peer to Contribute to their Treatment Team
- o Applying a Range of Strategies to Problem-Solving
- o Showing Independence and Initiative in Identifying and Solving Problems
- o Using Critical Thinking Skills to Solve Problems
- o Resolving Peer Concerns in Relation to Care and Recovery Needs
- o Using SWOT Analysis and Other Tools to Solve Problems

Section 5 – Initiative and Enterprise
- o Adapting to New Situations
- o Developing a Strategic, Creative and Long-Term Vision
- o Being Creative
- o Translating Ideas into Action
- o Initiating Innovative Solutions

Section 6 – Self-Management
- o Having a Personal Vision and Goals
- o Articulating Own Ideas and Vision
- o Translating Ideas into Action
- o Evaluating and Monitoring One's Own Recovery Health
- o Having Knowledge and Confidence in One's Own Ideas and Visions
- o Developing and Maintaining a Personal Recovery Plan
- o Developing Cultural Awareness
- o Establishing and Using Peer Networks
- o Professional Development
- o Credentialing
- o Continuous Education
- o Planning the Use of Resources, Including Time Management
- o Performance Evaluation

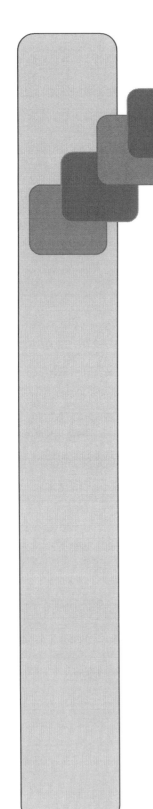

Section 1

Universal Essential Skills

INTERVIEWING 101

Preparing for the Interview

Research the Organization

This will help you answer and come up with questions while standing out from other candidates. It is important that you learn as much as you can about where you are applying. There are several available resources for researching potential employers and many ways to go about preparing for an interview, and eventually, a job.

Seek Background Information

• Use tools such as Vault, Glassdoor, The Riley Guide or just perform a good internet search for an overview of the organization and its industry profile

• Visit the organization's website to ensure that you understand the position and company in full

• Review and understand the organization's background and mission statement

• Read recent press releases for knowledge on projected growth and stability

Get Perspective

• Review trade and business publications, news and press releases
• Why do you want to work for this organization?

• Glimpse into their industry standing: How they compare with other organizations

Develop a Question List

Most interviews will contain a portion where the interviewer invites you to ask questions. Though it might seem positive to not have any questions, as it implies you are well-educated on the job, there should always be a few questions to ask at the end of your interview. These questions should not be about payment, vacation days, personal time or anything that is meant to strictly benefit you. There will be time for those questions later.

- Prepare to ask about the organization and position based on your research

- Engage in a discussion with your interviewer to show you are prepared

How do your skills and qualifications compare to the requirements of the job?

Learn the Job Description: take time to learn the knowledge, skills and abilities required. If you are unsure what some of the qualifications or terminology used mean, remember that the internet is a wonderful resource.

Understand the Hierarchy: determine where the position you seek fits within the organization. For example, an entry-level position typically means a position that does not require previous experience. This is different from a supervisor position, which requires previous experience – possibly many years.

Compare and Contrast: compare what the employer is seeking against the qualifications you know you have. Do you meet the qualifications? If you are not sure, it might be worth it to ask the company's Human Resources department or just apply anyway.

Responsible Preparation and What to Wear

Business Profession: Average business attire, such as a suit and professional, polished shoes, is always best. It is recommended to own at least one well-fitting suit.

Err on the Formal Side: If instructed to dress business casual, use your best judgment. For those that dress in a masculine fashion, a suit and tie is always a reliable and safe option. Basic, polished dress shoes that match your belt are recommended. A dress with a nice cardigan or blazer is a safe feminine option. Try to avoid a very-high-heeled shoe, or shoes with open toes or without backing. Basic pumps, a kitten heel or dress boots are recommended.

Cleanliness: Make sure your clothes are neat, clean and wrinkle-free. A dirty shirt or crumpled tie will stand out – and not in a good way. Hair should be clean and neat. If you have long hair, sometimes it is best to pull it back for an interview.

It is best to have the following handy:

• Extra copies of your resume and professional references on quality paper, without creases or wrinkles. It is best to buy a simple, but untarnished, folder to carry your paper work. If your resume is more than one page, staple the pages in the top, left corner.

• A notepad or professional binder, and working pen (with one or two back up pens)

• Information you need to complete an application. This can include past employers, including their names, address of place of employment, date range spent there, contact information and the reason why you left

• If relevant, include a portfolio with writing samples of your work or written references

Importance of Non-Verbal Communication

This applies to you *and* the interviewer. Notice how they react to you when you talk or share an anecdote, and make sure you have appropriate reactions as well.

Be Mindful: Nonverbal communication, such as facial expression and eye contact, can speak volumes. If you have a mouth that naturally turns down and can cause you to look unintentionally grumpy, try to smile a lot. Make sure you are properly rested to avoid yawning, or worse, nodding off during an interview. Falling asleep will make it highly unlikely you will receive an invitation to return. If you are a smoker, please try not to smoke before the interview. If you do, wash your hands with soap and water or use antibacterial sanitizer to help remove the smell.

Start the Moment You Walk in the Door: First, arrive at least fifteen minutes early. Remember that waiting room behaviors may be reported. It is best to sit politely and peruse any company magazines or brochures they may have in the waiting room. Once in the waiting room, your cell phone should be on silent or off. An exception is if they want you to fill out a paper application and you need to look at your phone for information. It cannot hurt to double-check with the receptionist to make sure it is okay to use your phone for that purpose.

Show Your Confidence: Smile, shoulders back, stand up straight, establish eye contact and present a firm handshake. Do not be afraid to be yourself, just be the most professional version of you.

Avoid Visible Nervousness: Sit up straight, yet comfortably. Be aware of anxious gestures, such as nail-tapping. If you are nervous while waiting, try taking a deep breath for seven seconds and exhaling for ten seconds.

Pay Attention: Maintain good eye contact while addressing all aspects of an interviewer's questions. It is better for you to ask them to repeat a question than to not answer fully.

Try to be Positive: Manage how you react, and project a positive image. Remember to smile. Avoid using sarcasm or telling odd anecdotes or inappropriate jokes. Even if you do not feel like the interview is going well, keep doing your best. Worst case scenario is that this will be good practice for another job interview.

Follow Up

Many interviews wrap up with "Do you have any questions?" and the interviewer is going to appreciate your inquires. Also, always get a business card from the interviewer before you leave.

Bring a List of Questions: You may say, "In preparation for today's meeting, I took some time to write down a few questions." They might have answered your questions throughout the interview, so it is good to have a few specific questions tucked away. Questions are good to have, so do not be afraid to ask.

Be Strategic: Cover information not discussed or clarify a previous topic. Examples are:

- o In your opinion, what is the best part of the job?
- o What do you consider the most important criteria for success in this position?
- o Why do you like your job?
- o How will my performance be evaluated?
- o What are the next steps in the hiring process?

Thank You Email: Send an email to your interviewer(s) within 24-48 hours thanking them for their time.

Hello/Good Morning/Afternoon [Interviewer's name],

Thank you for taking the time to speak with me about the [position/job title] at [company name]. It was wonderful to meet you.

I am excited about your opportunity. After our conversation on [date] I am confident in my ability to fulfill the job requirements. If you require further information or references, please feel free to contact me via email or at [insert your phone number]. I look forward to hearing from you.

Thank you,

[Your name]

You

Sharing Your Story

When sharing your story during recovery, consider the following things during job interviews:

1. Be Consistent: In this era of easily-accessible internet, your prospective employer might find time to look you up online. If you do not wish to address your recovery during the job hunt, make sure your social media presence is consistent with your desire for privacy. Also, if you have questionable content that you cannot (or prefer not to) remove from the World Wide Web, then everything available needs to be as professional as possible. This could mean strengthening your privacy settings or editing existing content. Hiring managers are going to understand that you lead a life, so a picture of you out to dinner or at a sports game is okay. However, if the picture includes you smoking or drinking an alcoholic beverage, those could easily be considered in bad taste. Interviewers and hiring managers live lives too, and they might be okay with your outside-of-work-behavior. However, better to err on the side of caution and keep your internet presence professional.

2. Handling the Stigma: Choosing to open up about what you went through can help combat preexisting notions people hold about what it means to struggle with substance use disorder. This is aspirational, and it comes at a critical time in the evolution toward viewing addiction as a disease instead of a moral failing. What you decide to share is a personal decision. A potential employer cannot hold recovery against you, but where you are in the process is important. You do not have to share your recovery process and it is ultimately up to you to handle this conversation. If you would rather avoid the topic, that is fine. Honesty is always a good policy, so try to stay truthful.

3. Focus on Your Strengths: You had to scale hypothetical icy mountains and swim oceans of emotions against the current to reclaim yourself. That takes energy, bravery and a burgeoning strength you might not have known you were capable of. You are stronger and braver than you think you are. Even if sobriety was not by choice (medical reason, intervention), you still did it. If you choose to share your story, focus on detailing the strengths you gained because of your experience, and how those strengths will benefit your prospective employer. You do not have to consider recovery your only strength – recovery does not define you, and you have other wonderful qualities to talk about as well.

4. Be Prepared: If your resume reveals significant gaps, during which you were in active addiction, struggling or in treatment, be prepared for questions regarding unemployment. Depending on how significant these gaps are, you may feel pressure to disclose some information about your recovery. This is a reality you need to plan for ahead of time. What you say is up to you.

5. Be Honest: You own your story – it does not belong to anyone else. You can be honest, but it does not mean you have to share everything. You do not owe anyone any of your story. If you choose not to share, fight the urge to fabricate explanations for things such as gaps in employment. Lying is never good practice and it needs to be avoided. Find a way to bring the conversation back to your strengths instead.

6. The Law is on Your Side: The Federal Americans with Disabilities Act prohibits employers from discriminating against hiring people with substance use disorders, as long as they are not currently using illegal drugs. Once hired, you may request reasonable accommodation under the law for medical care and rehabilitation efforts. Your Human Resources department is likely going to be the best place for you to find assistance.

7. Find the Right Fit: Where are you in your recovery? You must consider your own needs first. This is applicable to life in general, including when applying for a new job. It is important to find a supportive environment. If you are not ready for a recovery-oriented position, that is okay. *You have to take care of yourself.* That is always the most important rule.

The Secret Weapon That Anyone Can Bring to an Interview to Stand Out
by Jennifer E Little-Fleck

I recently read some bad advice from a supposed career expert. The job seeker was asking whether or not he should prepare interview materials other than some clean copies of his resume.

The answer went like this:

"Well, some industries are known for preparing presentations or portfolios of their work or examples of previous projects, but it's not for everyone. Mostly for people in sales or marketing. You probably don't need one."

My jaw hit the ground. I couldn't believe I was actually reading an exchange in which an expert was telling someone not to go the extra mile—telling him to not to do something that would help him stand out.

And if there's one thing all recruiters agree on, it's that you need to take every opportunity to stand out among all the other talented candidates. While there are lots of different ways to do that, one way I've discovered works wonders is to put together an interview portfolio. No matter what industry you're in or job title you're after, it almost always impresses.

An Interview Portfolio Is What Exactly?

An interview portfolio consists of six main parts: an introduction, a professional background summary, STAR behavioral examples, awards and recommendations, sample solution(s), and a closing page. While the content will be similar to what's on your resume, the portfolio takes it a step further to "show and tell" your skills with specific examples. Your goal is to get the hiring manager to visualize you solving problems for him.

---

[1] Little-Fleck, J. Retrieved from https://www.themuse.com/advice/the-secret-weapon-that-anyone-can-bring-to-an-interview-to-stand-out

And I Should Have One Because…

Creating an interview portfolio does three things for you that can skyrocket you past other candidates. First, it shows that you're serious, that you do your homework before an interview, and that you don't take the process lightly. You're in it to win it. That goes a long way with both HR recruiters and hiring managers because they want to not only *see* that you want a job, but also that you want *this* job. The portfolio demonstrates enthusiasm for the position. Because <u>employee turnover's costly</u>, the powers that be want to get it right the first time—meeting with someone who is obviously excited for the opportunity can make all the difference.

Along with demonstrating your enthusiasm, a portfolio prepares you for the interview better than any other method out there. Here's the thing: To a recruiter, it looks like a wonderful showcase of your skills and accomplishments, but for you—it's a cheat sheet! Getting nervous and forgetting to say something impressive, or worse, saying something that doesn't sound as good out loud as it did in your head is normal. Taking time to write out some examples of your brilliance ahead of time will aid you in having a <u>successful interview</u>.

On top of all that, this physical packet serves as a tangible reminder of your talents. You're giving yourself an edge because now the hiring manager can quickly reference your skills and accomplishments.

Does This Really Work?

Yes, but don't just take it from me. There are many people who have been doing this type of preparation for years. Take Kelly Stamerra, a senior hospital pharmaceutical sales representative, for example, who says, "It started out as just a way to look and sound more credible when I was just starting out, but after a while I realized not only was it keeping me on track, but it directed the conversation. I felt so comfortable discussing the information I had put in there because I had taken the time to think about it, so I never went down a rabbit hole."

The result? "I call it my lucky presentation," Stamerra explains. "Hands down I would not have gotten the jobs I did without it. As I continued to apply for promotional positions, it made me sound polished and professional and I quickly moved into specialty positions. It is my security blanket. Honestly, I would feel naked going into an interview without it!"

What Is A Career Portfolio?

The Elements of a Portfolio typically include:

- Resume
- Cover Letter
- References Page

Optional elements include:

- Copies of Letters of Recommendation
- Copies of Educational Certificates, Certifications, Licenses and Degrees
- Copies of Awards, Honors, or other Recognition Items
- Samples of Work or Summaries of Projects (This can include a report you wrote, a print out of a spreadsheet you designed, a flow chart, a test you took, a project summary, a flowchart, etc.)
- Positive employment evaluations
- A personalized letter of recommendation from your Peer Supervisor/Mentor/Sponsor (if you joined AA, NA, GA, etc.)
- A sample of a completed Service Plan
- A qualification support letter from a Peer Recovery Trainer
- Peer letters of support

TELL ME ABOUT YOURSELF

Answer This Job Interview Question: Tell Me (or Us) About Yourself[2]

By Laura DeCarlo

While this is often among the first questions asked at the start of the interview, the goal of the interview is not to become best friends. The goal is to determine if you are a good fit for their job.

This question may come disguised as, *"What should I know about you?"* or they might say, *"What would you like me to know about you."*

Like the *"Why should we hire you?"* question, this is an opportunity to market yourself, presenting yourself as the solution (right candidate) for their problem (a job to fill). So, tell them the things that emphasize how your accomplishments and experience make you an ideal candidate for the job you are seeking.

Answer the *Real* Question

You probably find yourself wondering, "What is it they really want to know?"

Excellent thought!

Since this is usually among the first questions asked, they typically are interested in a quick summary of whom you are and what you have accomplished, related to this job opening. They want to understand how well you fit into *this* position.

So, tell them how well you fit, using the 2-part answer, below. But, don't spend more than 60 seconds answering this question.

Perhaps, ask for clarification.

To ensure that you provide the information they want, you might wish to start your response with a question of your own, like this --

---

[2] Decarlo, L. Retrieved from https://www.job-hunt.org/job_interviews/answering-tell-me-about-yourself-question.shtml

"I would be glad to. Could you give me an idea of the type of information you would like to know?"

By starting this way, you can direct your answer better and be more conversational.

What You *Don't* Tell Them

I call this question a "spider web" because if you simply tell someone about yourself without planning or context to the target job for which you are there to interview, you could give away all kinds of information that leaves them with the impression that you are:

1. Over-qualified
2. Under-qualified
3. Ditzy or naive
4. Unprepared for the interview (so not really very interested)
5. Simply a risk for the company

Most people talk about what they know, ramble on about where they live, kids, likes/dislikes, but, remember, THIS IS A JOB INTERVIEW.

The sole purpose of this interview is to see if you are a fit for the employer; a fit for the job!

Therefore, your goal is to avoid answers that give away personal information about yourself. An employer isn't going to select to hire you because you have such cute children, a wonderful husband or wife, or interesting hobbies.

How to Prepare for This Job Interview question

Before you ever go to an interview, you need to *KNOW YOURSELF* in terms of qualifications for the job and match for the company.

To know this you should:

- Carefully review the job description to note where you meet or exceed the requirements, and
- Research the company, and

- Identify, catalog, list, and review your expertise, strengths, and unique value, and
- Practice, practice, practice so you sound natural and confident.

Then, you will be ready to put yourself in the employer's shoes and emphasize what will make you stand out for the company and for the job.

The Two-Part Answer to Tell Me/Us About Yourself

This is *not* an invitation to tell your life story or share any secrets about your current or former employers. Put yourself in the employer's shoes. Emphasize what will make you stand out as qualified for the company and for the job.

Break your answer to this question into two parts:

1. How/why you are qualified.

Summarize what you have done that qualifies you for this opportunity. Don't recite what is on your resume or job application, but don't assume that the interviewers, who may have been interviewing several candidates, remember your qualifications.

Present the most significant highlights, the ones that would be most relevant to this job. These are the qualifications that make it clear that you are a very good candidate for the job.

2. Why you have applied.

Focus on advancing your career. Stay away from reasons that are not clearly career-related. Emphasize the opportunity to move forward in your career *without* saying that you are dead-ended in your current job.

Avoid the purely personal reasons. Do NOT say:

- You want to work closer to home because your kids sometimes get out of school early and you want to be able to be there with them, or
- You are too tired from the long commute to enjoy life, or
- Your boss is a jerk and you want a better job.

This is where you must tread very carefully and not say anything that might be interpreted as trashing your current/former employer.

Sixty-Second Elevator Pitch

What Is An Elevator Pitch?

The term "elevator pitch" refers to the amount of time you would have if you were in an elevator with someone riding from the bottom of the building to the top of an average building. The pitch is approximately a sixty-second spiel to tell someone who you are and why they should want to hire you. A good pitch will allow you to explain precisely who you are and what you have to offer.

Elevator speeches are good for much more than just catching someone in a small, enclosed space –You never know who you might run into at a cocktail party, the movies, the pharmacy, an airport or wherever else you may frequent.

How to Write an Elevator Pitch

For example, let us say you are a sales employee and you just walked into an elevator with the CEO of a huge company. You want to change your job and he is *just* the person for you to speak to about joining his team. The doors are shut and no one else is present. You have about sixty seconds to convince him to not only listen to you, but also to consider you as a potential employee.

Start with an introduction and an interesting anecdote. Can you tell a story about what you do in a way that is interesting? Do you have an accomplishment that you can explain? For example:

"I started as an intern in 2014. Since then, I worked my way up to a Team Lead and in the past two years, I helped lead my team soar to the number one spot in sales."

What story would you tell?

_____
_____
_____
_____

What is your objective? What is your goal?

_____
_____
_____

What makes you the best at what you do? Why are you the perfect candidate? Can you provide an entertaining anecdote or a serious story that tells how you helped someone with your product?

_____
_____
_____
_____
_____

You just told a great story, but besides the entertainment value or the seriousness, why should your audience care?

_____
_____
_____
_____
_____

You are capable of providing a perfectly acceptable elevator pitch. You can tell your audience what you do, why your job is important, hook them in with what you plan to do next for their company, and, most importantly, you can tell them who you are. Even if you do not feel confident, sometimes you just need to pretend. It is not always easy, but it is highly encouraged to practice your confidence. Prepare your pitch in a mirror, or have friends or family listen to you. If you pretend to believe in yourself, you will likely eventually truly feel that way.

The nice thing about an elevator pitch is that it is short, sweet and to the point. Make sure you have a good understanding of your audience. Once you get the basics figured out, you should be able to use it on just about anyone, in any situation - as long as you always tailor your hook to your specific audience.

Elevator Pitch Mistakes To Avoid

Now that you know what to do in your elevator pitch, we shall briefly discuss practices that you will benefit from avoiding.

- **Speed of Speaking**

Remember to choose words wisely. Avoid attempting to cram fifteen minutes of information into one minute of someone's time.

- **Using Highly Technical Terms, Acronyms or Slang**

You want your pitch to be easily understood by *any* audience. That means try to avoid using words that will confuse the average person. The last thing you want is for your audience to feel dumb. People do not always understand what you mean. For example, you can say "I saw a new PCP". In the medical field, that refers to your Primary Care Physician. To others, it might refer to an illegal substance. You do not need to use big words to have a big impact.

- **Stay Focused**

Keep your pitch clear and focused. However, if you feel that some small talk might benefit you, then go for it. Understanding your audience is a big part of this. If you are losing your audience, change your speech.

- **Avoid Sounding Robotic**

Having an easy, approachable, conservatively-casual-style to your pitch will get you much farther than an overly-rehearsed monologue approach. It should be the start of a conversation, not a forced presentation. You do not want to sound like you are reading from a brochure. You want to sound genuine. The best way to sound genuine, is to be yourself. Again, practice so you will be comfortable.

- **Retrieving Contact Information**

If the conversation appears to go well, then do not hesitate to ask for a business card. If they do not have one handy, ask for their name. You can possibly find them through LinkedIn or the company website. If you have a business card of your own, that is even better. Feel free to offer them one.

- **Missing an Opportunity**

It will do nothing for you to have a great elevator pitch if you never use it. However, if you feel uncomfortable, anxious or unable to do your pitch, it is okay. There will be other opportunities. There always are.

Important Factors to Include in Your Pitch

- Your name, followed by something that differentiates you from your peers (major/degree, athlete, veteran) and/or establishes a relationship (graduate of same college, from the same home town, etc.).
- Your ultimate goal or general career interest. This will assist your audience with helping you, or possibly connect you to someone beneficial.
- Explain how you pursue your interest. Show with examples of things that are already completed. Do not just say, "I have always wanted be a lawyer," but rather "I completed pre-law as an undergrad and interned with Smith and Jones."
- Why you are qualified. Demonstrate your qualifications by sharing leadership examples, work experience, achievements, expertise, skills and strengths. You can include this as an aside while explaining another one of your assets.
- A question, or request for assistance. Consider giving your audience two options for ways they might help you. For example, "If your company offers internships, I would love to apply. Who should I send my resume to?"

Perfecting Your Pitch

- Hello, it is a pleasure to meet you. My name is _____ and I am a trained _____. I am interested in a career as a Peer Recovery Specialist because _____ (demonstrate your truthful and genuine commitment, dedication, and passion). I am involved with/in_____ (what have you done in the community to serve those you want to work with, what are you currently doing). I am experienced with _____ (group facilitation, service planning, mentoring). I also have performed as a _____ (mention applicable experienced here) with _____ and I truly enjoy _____. Also, I can _____ (data base management, time management, systems you know how to use, etc.)

Peer Support Specialist Interview Questions and Answers

1. Why do you want this peer support specialist position?

People want to hire people who are passionate about the job, so you should have an honest and poignant answer prepared about why you want the position. Identify a few key factors that make the role a great fit for you (for example, "I strive in customer support because I love helping others. Plus, the satisfaction that comes from helping someone solve a problem is a great feeling."), then share why you love this particular company (for example, "I've always been passionate about assisting others. Your company has made amazing strides in this field and in the community.).

2. Have you ever learned from mistakes in the peer support specialist position?

The example you share should be fairly inconsequential, unintentional, and, ultimately, result in a learned lesson. An easy example of this is a time when you went ahead without group assistance, but you were assigned to a group project that was meant to be collaborative.

3. What challenges are you looking for in this peer support specialist position?

The best way to answer questions such as this is to discuss how you would like to be able to effectively utilize your skills and experience if, and when, you are hired for the job. You can also mention that you are motivated by challenges, are able to effectively meet goals, and have the flexibility and skills necessary to handle a challenging job. Think of examples where you had to be resourceful and think outside the box.

4. Can you describe typical work for peer support specialist?

Interviewers will likely want to know what you do while working. Always consider the position you are applying for and how your current or past roles relate to it. The more you can connect your past experience with the job opening, the more successful you will be answering the questions. Sometimes applicants will offer information about how they are often late because they have to drive a pet to doggie daycare or like to take a long lunch break to go for a stroll when the weather is nice. Keep your answers focused on work and show the interviewer that you are organized and efficient. Displaying an appropriate appearance will help you with this aspect.

5. What is your biggest weakness?

This is always a tough question, as it requires a very delicate balance. You cannot say you do not have one, because you do – we all do. Avoid explaining your fault to the interviewer by offering up a personal weakness that is really a strength ("I work too hard"). Do not be so honest you harm your chances ("I'm not a morning person so I am usually a few minutes late. If I don't stop for a coffee on my way in, I'm useless!"). Think of a smaller flaw, such as, "I sometimes get sidetracked by small details that need editing", or "I am still somewhat nervous about public-speaking, but I really want to improve." Make it clear you are aware of the problem and you are doing your best to grow as a person and eliminate the issue.

6. Why should the we hire you?

This is the part where it all comes together. You need to link your skills, experience, education and your personality to the requirements for the position. You need to know the job description and it is best to back up those details with actual examples of how you are a perfect fit. Unfortunately, it is always possible that you may not have the same skills, experience or qualifications as the other candidates. You need to figure out what makes you *you*. Why makes you stand out? Energy, passion and a sense of humor are great traits. People are attracted to someone who is charismatic, and show energy, and who love what they do. As you explain your compatibility with the job and company, be sure to portray yourself as that motivated, confident and energetic person that is more than ready to commit to the cause of the company. Also, big smile can go a long way.

7. **What do you know about our company?**

It is highly recommended you follow these tips:

a) Go to the company website and read the "About Us" section and "Careers" sections, at the least.

b) Visit the company's LinkedIn page (note: you must have a LinkedIn account — it is free to sign up and an account is a good idea) to view information about the company

c) Do an internet search for a keyword search phrase, such as "press releases", followed by the company name. Unfortunately, depending on the position, you might want to also search for the company followed by the word, "scam". Often recruiters have a certain amount of contacts and resumes to obtain and you might just be another number to them. This is not always the case, of course.

Keep in mind that reciting every fact you learned is not necessary, but it is good to have a few key details memorized. At the very least, try to know the following:

I. What type of product or service the company sells

II. How long the company has been in business

III. The company's mission statement and how it relates to your values or personality

8. **Why do you want to work here?**

Every organization has its strong points, as does every individual. These are aspects you should highlight in your answer. For example, if the company emphasizes integrity with customers, then mention that you would like to be in such a team because you believe in and understand the importance of integrity. It does not have to be a lie. In the case that your values are not in line with the ones by the company, ask yourself if you would be happy working there. If you are aware of the company culture and realize that there is a potential personal dilemma you might end up facing, you ought to think twice. The best policy is to be honest with yourself and avoid convincing yourself that a position is right for you when it is not. Be honest with the interviewer with what in the company culture that motivates you. It is okay if you realize a job is not a good match for you and do not want to proceed.

9. Do you find the salary attractive?

We all know the salary is an important factor regarding your interest in this job, but it should not be the overriding reason for your interest. If it is, the interviewer does not need to know that.

10. Do you have any questions to ask us?

As we mentioned before, you should have some questions prepared. Never ask about money, vacation time, bonuses and other perks, etc. If something comes up naturally, then it can be okay to ask. For example, you might get a tour of the building and they will show you the gym. It is okay to ask if you will be allowed to use the gym. Usually, information like that will be offered to you.

Presenting Your Weakness As A Strength

Yes, you *do* have a weakness. We all have weaknesses. It is a part of being human. One of the worst answers to this question is, *"I don't have any weaknesses,"* or *"I can't think of any relevant weaknesses."*

An answer like the above exhibits a lack of self-awareness or just plain dishonesty. Those are not positive interview traits. Focus on the weaknesses you have overcome, particularly weaknesses that had an impact on your ability to do your job. For example, maybe you preferred to work alone, but at your last job you realized how beneficial working in groups can be – the sharing of ideas, the brainstorming, the comradery – are all things you realized are great. Now you like working solo and in groups.

Prepare to Offer More than One Weakness

You may be asked for a second, and even a third weakness, so be prepared and use the two-part answer:

1. **The confession** of the weakness, and...
2. **The recovery** -- how you learned from your weakness, found a way to benefit from it, or (more risky) the plan you have for recovery from said weakness.

Be sure to present these weaknesses in terms of how they impact the employer.

After the Interview

The job market can be a tough, competitive place with hundreds of people vying for the same one position. Creating an impressive resume to grab the attention of your prospective employer is just the beginning. There are several formalities and procedures underway, it might take some time for the letter to find its way into your hands or inbox. It might take ten, twenty, thirty or more attempts to get a job. Sometimes a friendly reminder will prove beneficial to you. As previously mentioned, sending a kind email after an interview is a great way to start. However, it is important that you know when to send an email and what to write in it. Send the email within a day or two after your interview. A poorly written or timed email can botch your chances of getting your hands on that much-coveted job. Here are some emailing tips:

3. *Always spellcheck!* Some people do not notice typos. For others, it is a deal breaker. When in doubt, look up a word's meaning. For example, if you do not know the difference between "accept" or "except" consult a dictionary.
4. Avoid contractions. It is better to say, "do not" than "don't", "cannot" than "can't" and so on.
5. Avoid clichés like the plague (that is actually a cliché – do not use it)
6. Use phrases correctly. "Should of", "could of", "would of" should all be "should have," "could have, " and, "would have".

7. Please do not use strange abbreviations. Spell out the word "because" instead of using the word "cause". While some people might understand you meant "because", the word "cause" has a whole separate meaning.
8. Watch out for your verb tenses. You do not want to describe your position at your current job by saying "Attended the cash register", followed by "Supervising ten employees." "Attended" and "Supervising" are different tenses. Some people might not notice or care. But there are some people who will find that to be a deal-breaker.

Emailing when you do not receive a response:

If it has been more than one or two weeks and you have not heard back, it is okay to send an email reminding the recruiter or interviewer that you are still interested in the job.

Email asking for time to think on the offer:

Congratulations! You impressed the interviewer and got a job offer. If you need time to think about it, it is okay to let them know that. Always start by expressing your gratitude. Then, offer a time frame and see if they are okay with allowing you said time to think it over. The time frame you request should not be longer than a week.

Email to accept an offer:

Congratulations again! All that you need to do now is to accept it. Again, gratitude should come first. Make sure you give them a firm answer and use future-speak, such as "I look forward to my first day working with you," as opposed to confusing tensed phrasing, such as "I'd really look forward to when I'm starting the job."

Email to decline an offer:

In case you get a better offer than the one you already have at hand, or the pay is insufficient, or the commute is too far, still take time and write an email to decline the offer. You never know when you might want to reapply for this job and it is highly recommended you avoid burning any and all theoretical bridges.

The follow-up emails that you write after an interview should be extremely professional and precise. This is what will make a positive impression on the recruiters and have them remember you for all the right reasons.

THE CELEBRATION

The term "celebrating" might bring to mind champagne, a night out, and possibly back-tracking through Stages of Relapse, but celebration can take on many forms. Try these tips:

Eat A Wonderful Meal with Friends and Family

Do you know that new restaurant you have been wanting to try? Check it out! Maybe it is a little pricey – you can always give it a try and just get an appetizer. Feel like staying at home? Order take out! Do you want an ice cream sundae? Go for it! Treat yourself to something you want, but remember food is never meant to be a replacement for your compulsion. It is very easy to replace one addiction for another, but you can still enjoy yourself.

Go Somewhere Fun

Think back to your childhood for inspiration. Get some friends together for a board game night, or even a game of Capture the Flag. Maybe try amusement park, sports stadium, glass blowing, a painting night or music festival. If you want to stay in, that is okay, too. Sometimes Netflix, Hulu, newest edition of US Weekly, or a good book will satisfy your need for a fun time.

Buy Yourself a Gift

Do you know that pair of shoes you have had your eye on for quite a while? Or that dent in your car you have been meaning to have fixed? If you have the time and funds, treat yourself.

AVOIDING THE PITFALL

A new job or a promotion is often a time for celebration, which, for most people in recovery, was at one time synonymous with indulging in drugs or alcohol. A promotion can be a double-edged sword – a confidence-builder as well as a temptation to use their increased financial resources for drugs or alcohol.

In many cases, there is not a need for those in recovery to turn down a job offer or a promotion to protect their sobriety. Following a significant change in income, one may benefit from a financial advisor or speaking to someone at the bank about setting up a savings account. If there are debts that need to be paid, do not delay in resolving those debts. The interest on loans and credit cards will add up. You might not be able to imagine the day you are debt free, but it is cathartic to try. It is a wonderful feeling.

TRANSITIONING AND ANXIETY

Do no overthink the new job. You were instructed with specifics for your first day, such as where and when to report, and to whom. Focus on that as you head into your first day of work. You might be part of a training class with multiple people in the same figurative shoes as you. That is not always the case, but do not worry. You do not know who your friends are yet, you do not know who you can trust yet, you do not know the ins and outs of every aspect of the job yet. The key word here is "yet", because you will meet people, you will learn the job and you will first and foremost make it through day one.

Remember Why They Hired You

You were hired because you are the best person for the position. The interviewer and additional staff decided that your skills, your experience, your strengths, your talents, and your character make you the perfect person. You might not realize how great you are, but someone noticed and they knew you were the right candidate.

Fear of failure is real, but it does not mean it is realistic. Sometimes the fear of failure will make you want to hurry up and fail so you can get the experience over with. Make sure to work to deliver what people expect.

Fear can also make you hold yourself back. Maybe you avoid voicing your opinion in case it gets you noticed. Maybe others will disagree with your opinion. Avoid building walls around yourself. Remember, you are always going to be thinking about what you said or did for a much longer period of time than others will. If you make a mistake, it might get noticed, but it is likely no one will care about it as much as you do (this obviously depends on what kind of mistake is made, as something like accidentally deleting all files in the database might have serious consequences). These thoughts can stifle creativity and innovation, while turning work into a struggle, and prevent you from completing accomplishment. You will find you are more likely to fail by resisting than you are by engaging.

Failure Is Not the Enemy

It happens to the best of us. You made mistakes before, and you are still here. You failed before, and you learned from it. Did you ever touch a burner on the stove to see if it was on? I bet you learned never to do that again, once you developed a nice burn blister. In order to learn, you need to make mistakes. Failure is not what you should be fearing. Not being willing to try in the first place is far worse.

Computer Literacy

THE LEARNING GOALS:

- Why Computers are Important
- How Computers Work
- Managing Files

The Importance of Computers

Computers are everywhere. Wherever your Peer Recovery certification takes you, it is imperative to have basic computer skills. Every employer requires basic computer knowledge in some form, whether you are employed in an office, recovery house, hospital or private sector. Computer literacy is a non-negotiable for employers today.

Computers allow for work to be completed at a faster pace, notes to be easily accessible through the workplace and for tasks to be managed with the click of a button. From basic note-taking to in-depth reporting, Peers must possess a basic knowledge of computers to perform necessary tasks.

How Computers Work

Computers have four basic functions:

1. **Accept Information/Input**. Data that you put into your computer

List things we use and ways to get information into a computer:

_____
_____
_____
_____
_____
_____
_____
_____

2. **Change Information/Process**. How your data changes

List ways we change information on a computer:

_____
_____
_____
_____
_____
_____
_____
_____

3. **Produce New information/Output**. Data that you can remove from your computer

List things we use to see the results of what we do with information:

_____
_____
_____
_____
_____
_____
_____
_____
_____
_____

4. Store New Information/Storage. Where data is stored

List places we store data on a computer:

_____
_____
_____
_____
_____
_____
_____
_____
_____

What are the advantages and disadvantages of each type of storage listed above?

_____
_____
_____
_____
_____
_____
_____
_____
_____

Keyboard Tips

Helpful Shortcut Keys
CTRL+C = _____
CTRL+V = _____
CTRL+X = _____

CTRL+A = _____

What are some other keyboard tips or shortcuts that you use?

_____
_____
_____
_____

Managing Files

It is important to keep your files organized. This will allow you to increase productivity and decrease errors or file mismanagement. Some key components to electronic file management are described below.

1. **Store all work-related files in one place.** Keep yourself organized and allow for files to be easily retrieved by storing all work-related documents in one location. Maintain proper protocol for your organization by following the policies and procedures as directed by your employer. For example, confidential Peer information should not be stored in personal files or on a personal computer. This will avoid putting privacy at risk. Utilize the software, file management or server to ensure ethical file management.
2. **Arrange files in a logical manner.** Label folders properly and concisely to assist with file organization. It might help to store files alphabetically, numerically, by name, by date, in ascending or descending order, as applicable to your organization. Use sub-folders so as not to clutter your electronic workspace.
3. **Be Specific.** Name your files using as much information as possible, without making them too lengthy or revealing private information. This will allow for ease, plus stress-free searching, when you need to access a file quickly. You want your file names to be short, but precise. For example, don't label a file "School Stuff" or "college classes Biology, Logic, Spanish", label it "[....] University/College" and then create a sub-folder for each class.
4. **Back up your files regularly.** Always back up your files so as not to lose information should your computer malfunction. Popular back-up tools include syncing to the Cloud, Microsoft OneDrive, Dropbox, Google Drive or Google Docs. Always be sure to follow your employer's policy as it relates to saving work-related files.

Check for Understanding

1. What is a Career Portfolio? Name 5 items that should be included in your career portfolio.
2. Name Important Aspects of Interview Etiquette.
3. What is an Elevator Pitch and why is it important?
4. Name the 4 key components of Electronic File Management.
5. What does it mean to present your weakness as a strength? Give an example.

Further Application

1. With a partner, ask and answer the ten Peer-related Interview Questions from pages 21-24.
2. Practice creating, saving, labeling and editing a file on your computer.
3. Create a Career Portfolio! Build and update your resume, write a cover letter, retrieve transcripts and certifications, gather a list of credible references and store all items in a safe place.

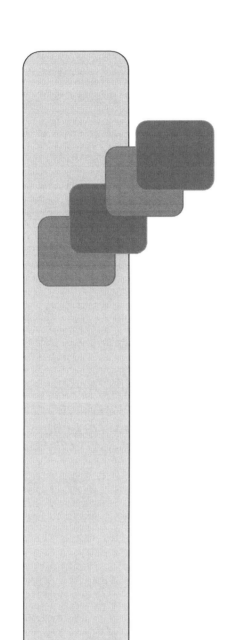

Section 2

Professional Communication

Strong, effective communication skills, whether verbal or non-verbal, are essential in the workplace. Speaking professionally allows you to capture your audience's attention and make your message known. Writing professionally tells the recipient that you want to be taken seriously. By writing professionally, you are leaving a lasting impression.

As a Peer, communication skills exceed far beyond the initial interview. Once you get your foot in the door, the real work begins. You must be able to build rapport with your Peer, professionally document interactions with Peers, effectively communicate questions or concerns to your Supervisor, as well as maintain a strong sense of self-awareness in your own recovery conversations.

PROFESSIONAL ETIQUETTE

What it means to be professional these days is not what it has meant for previous generations. We live in a new age where there is no longer always a standard workday, dress code or business code of conduct. For example, where there were once formal memos, now you might send out a text to your team members. Rather than pantyhose and pumps, flats and bare legs are acceptable. Thanks to smartphones and constant connectivity, gone are the days of interacting with co-workers solely between the hours of 9 a.m. and 5 p.m.

Professional boundaries have become very hazy in many workplaces. This can be particularly tricky if you are the manager and trying to maintain your professionalism with the people who report to you, especially if you developed a friendship. There are ways to make sure you are not crossing the line with your employees despite the intimate, connected work environment we find ourselves in these days. When in doubt, talk to your boss or Human Resources department about your concerns.

Here are tips for those trying to navigate the new definition of professionalism:

- **Social media management**

Facebook, Twitter, Snapchat, Instagram and more have allowed professional boundaries to disintegrate. If you were employed in the time before ever-present-updates on your co-worker's lives, you probably did not know much about what music they like, if they saw a movie lately or how your coworkers spent their weekend. Now if you are friends with them on Facebook, you can see updates about everything from where they ate dinner last night, to their relationship status.

Not too long ago, it was considered in poor taste to friend (or accept friend requests from) those who report to you, or to whom you report to. These days, some companies encourage employees to use social media as part of their job. For example, social media can be a good way to network with potential peers (receiving services) or promote the company. If everyone in your office posts and tweets for business purposes, it is probably fine to connect with employees and coworkers on social media. If you choose this particular interaction, make sure you keep it clean and professional. If your workplace frowns upon social media, check with your supervisor or Human Resources department to see what is and is not acceptable.

- **Socializing outside the office**

Today, many managers know that a little socializing outside the workplace can be a good thing. It can help you build trust with your team, and it can improve morale. Morale is crucial in maintaining staff. Most employees enjoy getting to know their boss a little bit better on a personal level. It is an opportunity for a boss to remind staff that they are a person, too. If you are a manager or arranging an event, try to keep it welcome to all of your staff. This means it is not recommended to have a bar-based get together, or anything that some might find unacceptable for personal or other reasons.

A boss can maintain professional boundaries at these events, too. Go ahead and talk about your family and your hobbies, as long as you avoid telling stories that might verge on being too personal. Listen as your employees talk about their weekend plans and ask questions that show your interest. Try to work the room and engage as many people as you can. You might learn something new and wonderful about many people that work with you.

WORKPLACE ETIQUETTE

Following the current rules of what most consider proper etiquette can make an incredible difference in how Peer Recovery Specialists are viewed by their peers. If peers feel valued by their Peer Recovery Specialists and have positive, honest interactions, they are more likely to be open to work with peers and receive services.

Here are some simple etiquette tips for Peer Recovery Specialists that can have a positive effect on individual (peer receiving services) relations and outcomes:

Stop, Look, Listen. This rule has great value in a Peer Recovery Specialist's work. Slow down and look around. Take in any red flags, or just general discomfort in others. In some instances, stop. In all cases, listen.

Maintain eye contact. Focus on the individual (peer receiving services) and not on the computer screen or the notebook in your lap. If your computer is placed in such a way that you must turn away from the peer, get a laptop or reconfigure the computer's placement. If you have trouble maintaining eye contact, try your best. If the peer does not want to maintain eye contact with you, that is okay. That is something you can eventually discuss but it is not a subject that needs to be addressed in the first few sessions.

When you ask critical questions, pay critical attention to the answers. Use good listening skills such as nodding, repeating key issues you heard and paraphrasing what was said. Avoid the urge to interrupt or finish the individual's sentence. If you accidentally interrupt, apologize and allow them to continue. If something is confusing or unclear, ask for clarification. You could miss valuable information. Remember, you are having an important conversation. You should treat it as such.

Practice professional meeting and greeting. Make your introduction warm, friendly and genuine. Remember, a smile will help put one at ease.

Use the individual's preferred name as soon as you can while adhering to individual (peer receiving services) privacy laws. Address people by their title and last name until you receive permission to call them by their first name. You may ask them if they have a name preference, such as a nickname. If someone has a name that is hard to pronounce, try your best. If it is too difficult, maybe the two of you can come up with a nickname.

Introduce yourself. This applies even if you are wearing a name badge (which you should be). Do not forget to give your title or position so individuals will know if they are speaking to a nurse, a technician or a housekeeper. If you have a nickname you would like to be called, please let them know.

Let the individual know what is going to happen next. For example, "I am going to check your blood pressure. Then you may have a seat in the waiting area until the doctor is ready to see you." Give them a time frame they can expect to wait. It is best if someone keeps an eye on how long the peer has been waiting and makes sure the individual is updated if it will be longer than initially advised.

Keep office differences under wraps. Not everyone in the office is best friends with (or even likes) their co-workers but this should never be your peer's problem. If employees cannot resolve the trouble between themselves, they need to take up their problem with the manager or Human Resources. It is in very poor taste to gossip to others in the office. You definitely should not make your issues with the other worker issues public.

DOS AND DON'TS

The Don'ts:

1.Don't "Reply All" to an email chain. This is especially true if your reply contains confidential information. Understand the differences—and repercussions—between "Reply" and "Reply All" to avoid humiliation. Unless you are instructed to reply all, it is recommended you avoid it. If it happens accidentally, learn from it.

2. Don't have a personal conversation at your desk. Go outside, to a break room, or chat on the phone after hours if you need to discuss your after-work issues that you might have with your best friend, sister, significant other, landlord (or anyone who is not related to work).

3. Don't bring your personal emotions into the office. This is more of a "Try Not To" than a "Don't". If it is unavoidable and you experience a tragedy, such as the death of a loved one, or are going through a hard time, speak to your Supervisor or Human Resources department. Sometimes bad and sad things happen and you have to just try your best.

4. Don't be afraid to ask questions. Despite how silly you think they seem, just ask. This way, you will avoid erroneously completing an entire project only to realize you did it all wrong.

5. Don't gossip about fellow coworkers, your peers or your boss. You are not hurting just yourself when you gossip, whether or not the gossip is true – if word gets back to the people you were talking about, you might never be able to undo the damage. Better yet, avoid being intolerable so that people do not gossip about *you*.

6. Do not insert emoticons or multiple exclamation points (if any) into work emails. Despite how relaxed your superiors might act, always be professional. The rule of thumb is to not use more than one explanation point, and that is only when necessary.

7. Do not wear weekend attire to the office. If your work has casual days, still dress respectably and avoid inappropriate or revealing outfits. If you are not sure if an outfit is appropriate, it probably is not. You can always ask a Supervisor if you are unsure. Casual days usually mean jeans and sneakers, maybe a t-shirt.

8. Don't React, Respond. Demonstrate respect, even if there is not much of an age difference between you and your supervisor. There may be times when you disagree with your boss or feel hurt by something they may say. It is important to remain respectful and learn the art of responding (which sometimes means waiting until things are calm, seeking advice from a colleague, taking time brainstorming ways to respond) versus reacting. If you truly believe them to be in the wrong, speak to their Supervisor or Human Resources.

9. Don't forget that at work socials, you are still at work. Be careful not to overdo it if alcohol is being served, know your limitations, and inform your Supervisor if an environment is a relapse risk. You can ask for no alcohol to be served at events you may be expected to attend. If that is not an option and you feel like you might be tempted, you might want to see if you can avoid the event. Be honest with yourself and your employer and do what is best for you.

10. Don't be nervous, but also don't overstep your boundaries. It is okay to express your opinions, but make sure to keep them G-rated. Be careful with political conversations and excuse yourself from any questionable conversations.

11. Don't forget an umbrella. Sitting in wet clothes all day is not typically fun. Keeping a pair of shoes under your desk is helpful, as well as a cardigan or blanket handy, if your employer allows it.

The Dos:

1. Do arrive early. You might not be remembered for answering your phone at 8:01 a.m., but you will be remembered if you show up late to work without prior approval. If you have an appointment before work, let your supervisor know, just in case you end up being late.

2. Do network with people. Working a job at a company you enjoy is great for meeting other people with similar interests and who share advice from their past experiences. You also might develop friendships.

3. Do establish and maintain professional boundaries. It is okay to laugh and chat during lunches and breaks, but when it is time to work, you need to work. Feel free to make friends at your workplace but proceed with caution. You will most likely have positive experiences with your co-workers, but that is not a guarantee.

4. Do establish a work-life balance. Your needs are very important. You might think you can do it all, but you cannot. You still need to rest, have fun, engage with your family and practice overall self-care (prayer, breaks, exercising, etc.).

5. Do be willing to help a coworker. This is a great opportunity to stand out and share your knowledge. It can be hard, but try not to be annoyed by their questions. If they are asking you for help that means they likely view you as a knowledgeable worker.

6. Do create a proper personal email address. Depending on your profession, you will most likely have to correspond with your coworkers after work and on weekends. Replace foxychick123 with a professional username, such as your first initial and last name. Ideally, this should be done before you even send out a resume. WeedGuy247 and Sexndrugs69 are not going to help your career.

7. Do take a chance to complete a new task. If you are asked to take on something new, it means those around you are recognizing your achievements and this will build confidence in your abilities. Do not assume you are being asked because they want you to do busy work. Also, remember you can ask your supervisor for additional work and more responsibility, but only if you feel comfortable taking on additional tasks,

8. Do be flexible. Sometimes a project calls for earlier or later hours. Try to be okay with adjusting your schedule accordingly.

9. Do work on holidays. Places like hospitals and residential treatment centers are usually open on the holidays. See what the policies are - Is there a rotating schedule? If so, take your turn at working a holiday from time to time without calling out sick if you really are perfectly fine. You will be rewarded in the long run for demonstrating responsibility. Some employers might need you to work Thanksgiving, but in return, you might have Christmas off.

10. Do watch your personal budget. Having an income does not mean you should spend all your money. Your bank might have resources, or you can consider speaking to a financial planner. Invest in your future.

11. Do make sure your ear buds are plugged in securely to your computer. First, make sure you are allowed to wear headphones. If you are, be mindful that your coworkers do not want to hear lyrics streaming from your Beyonce Pandora station (or if they do, that is their decision, not one that should be forced on them).

12. Do be open-minded. This refers to work and life. You never truly know someone else's story.

And finally...

13. Do always wear a smile. At least try, particularly when people are looking. Having a positive attitude about being at work will affect your job performance - significantly.

Listening and Understanding

Recognize & Use Person-Centered Language

Language has been around since creatures were able to make noise. Obviously, different animals have different ways of communicating. For example, when house cats communicate to each other it is often physical, with an about-to-pounce wiggle, a swat at a creature's bad behavior, or a hiss when they warn one to back off. A purr can be because of happiness, pain, and also associated with nursing and childbirth. Cats only meow to humans, because, through their evolution, it was discovered that mimicking the sound of a human baby crying (a "Meow") is the best way to evoke emotion.

Humans are not cats, and therefore it is not as easy to sum up our ways of communicating. Over time, humans developed words and now we have books full of them, in hundreds of languages, with words that have multiple meanings. Words can inform and comfort us, excite and thrill us, warm our hearts and inflame our desires. The old idiom, "Sticks and stones may break my bones, but words can never hurt me", is correct in the sense that words will not physically hurt you, but the mental pain and anguish can be very real.

Recovery-oriented, person-centered language is imperative to mental health and substance use recovery. It must be constructive and void of blame, while using verbiage that humanizes the individual instead of identifying them by their addiction or illness. The person in recovery is likely engrossed in getting better and their former behavior. They are already defining themselves as an addict, or something similar. They do not usually need to be reminded.

In order to be truly person-centered, word choice should be based on that which will meet that goal and fulfill for everyone involved in the conversation. Person-centred language helps tackle the stigma surrounding addiction. These preferred terms are meant to maintain dignity and respect for all individuals.

The purpose of person-centered language is to recognize the impact of spoken words on thoughts, paradigms, and behaviors, to ensure words do not diminish the uniqueness and intrinsic value of each person. Language presents a full range of thoughts, feelings, and experiences to be communicated while supporting the following principles:

Personhood
"This is a standing or status that is bestowed upon one human being by others in the context of relationship and social being. It implies recognition, respect and trust." -Kitwood, T.M.

Dignity and Respect
Positive conditions, created where one can live without fear of shame or ridicule; where people are treated with warmth and authenticity, listened to without judgment and are given opportunity for self-determination and self-expression are all crucial.

Acceptance and Understanding
Accepting each person with unconditional positive regard is essential. We are all flawed. Peer supporters should accept behavior as a form of communication that expresses unmet needs, varied emotions and help the person continue to enjoy basic personal freedoms.

Recognition and Individuality
Recognizing the individuality of each person's unique life experiences, personality, values, beliefs and opinions is a component of person-centered communication. Respect and incorporate these factors when support planning.

Relationships of Trust

It is vital to provide the conditions necessary to satisfy fundamental needs and create a climate for personal realization. This can be created by making a relationship based on trust. In a relationship of trust the person knows confidences are respected, choice and control are maintained, and they will not be abandoned.

Despite the fact that the process behind a recovery plan will likely be largely recovery-oriented, the translation of this process into the actual language of the planning document itself continues to be a core challenge. This can affect all providers who are committed to creating person-centered plans.

The following are useful guidelines to positive interactions in oral and written language:

- "Person-first" language should always be used to acknowledge that the compulsion or addiction is not as important as the person's individuality and humanity (for example, "a person in recovery" versus an "addict" or a "person with a substance use disorder" versus an "alcoholic coke-head" versus "an addict"). Therefore, the language used should be neither objectifying, nor stigmatizing. Person-first language does not mean that a person's problem is hidden or seen as irrelevant but is also is not to be the sole focus of any description about that person – that would be depersonalizing and derogatory and is no longer considered an acceptable practice. Do not define a person by the issues they are working hard to overcome.
- The language used should be is empowering and strengthening, avoiding the eliciting of pity or sympathy. Sympathy can be kind and well-meant, but it can cast people with disabilities in a passive, victim role and reinforce negative stereotypes. We should refer to "individuals who use medication as a recovery tool" as opposed to people who are "dependent on medication for clinical stability."
- Words such as "hope", "strength" and "recovery" are used frequently in documentation and delivery of services. Remember, there are other words out there that can be used to describe a person. Be careful to individualize each peer and to not lump them together.
- A peer recovery professional should try to interpret what might be considered negative within a strengths and resilience framework. This will

allow the peer to identify less with the limitations of their disorder. For example, an individual who takes their medication irregularly may be negatively- automatically perceived as "non-compliant," or "requiring monitoring to take meds as prescribed." At the same time, this individual can also be seen as "making use of alternative coping strategies such as exercise and relaxation to reduce reliance on medications" or could be praised for "working collaboratively to develop a contingency plan for when medications are to be used on an 'as-needed' basis." There is never just one way of looking at things. When it is up to you to document and report behavior, try to look at the issue as a whole, instead just from one viewpoint.

- Avoid labels that will typically yield minimal information regarding an individual's compulsion or addiction (such as, "Is a 33-year-old bipolar patient with..."). These can be considered catch-all labels and put a peer within a large generalization. Individual's needs are best captured by an accurate description of their functional strengths and limitations. While diagnostic terms may be required for other purposes (such as classifying the individual to support reimbursement from funders), their use should be limited elsewhere in the person-centered planning document.

Practice Effective Communication Skills

Since peer advocacy is a conversation or dialogue that happens between the Certified Peer Recovery Specialist and individual, the counselor needs certain communication skills to facilitate change. These include:

Attending

Effective attending puts Certified Peer Recovery Specialists in a position to listen carefully to what the individuals are saying or not saying. Attending refers to the various ways in that a Certified Peer Recovery Specialist can be with the peer physically and psychologically. Effective attending tells the individual that you are with them and that they can share safely with you. Effective attending also puts you in a position to listen carefully to what your individuals are saying.

The acronym SOLER[3] can be used to help you to show your inner attitudes and values of respect and genuineness towards a peer.

SOLER

S: Squarely face the individual. Adopt a bodily posture that indicates involvement with your peer. (A more angled position may be preferable for some- as long as you pay attention to the peer.) A desk between you and the individual may, for instance, can create a psychological barrier between you.

O: Open posture. Ask yourself to what degree your posture communicates openness and availability to the individual. Crossed legs and crossed arms may be interpreted as diminished involvement with the individual or even unavailability or remoteness, while an open posture can be a sign that you are open to the peer and to what he or she has to say.

L: Lean toward the individual (when appropriate) to show your involvement and interest. To lean back from them may convey the opposite message.

E: Eye contact with the person conveys the message that you are interested in what they have to say. If you catch yourself looking away frequently, ask yourself why you are reluctant to get involved with this person or why you feel so uncomfortable in his or her presence. Be aware of the fact that direct eye contact is not regarded as acceptable in all cultures.

R: Try to be relaxed or natural with the peer. Don't fidget nervously or engage in distracting facial expressions. The individual may begin to wonder what it is in himself or herself that makes you so nervous! Being relaxed can show that you are comfortable with using your body as a vehicle of personal contact and expression and for putting the person at ease.

---

[3] Egan, G. (2018, November). *The Egan Model and SOLER*. Retrieved from https://www.counsellingcentral.com/the-egan-model-and-soler/

Listening

Listening refers to the ability of Certified Peer Recovery Specialists to capture and understand the messages individuals communicate as they tell their stories, whether those messages are transmitted verbally or nonverbally.

Active listening involves the following four skills:

1. Listening to and understanding the individual's verbal messages.

When an individual tells you his or her story, it usually comprises a mixture of experiences (what happened to him or her), behaviors (what the peer did or failed to do) and affect (the feelings or emotions associated with the experiences and behavior). The Certified Peer Recovery Specialist must listen to the mix of experiences, behavior and feelings the peer uses to describe his or her problem situation. Also, try to hear what the individual is *not* saying.

2. Listening to and interpreting the individual's nonverbal messages.

Certified Peer Recovery Specialists should learn how to listen to and read nonverbal messages, such as bodily behavior (posture, body movement and gestures), facial expressions (smiles, frowns, raised eyebrows, twisted lips), voice related behavior (tone, pitch, voice level, intensity, inflection, spacing of words, emphases, pauses, silences and fluency), observable physiological responses (quickened breathing, a temporary rash, blushing, paleness, pupil dilation), general appearance (grooming and dress), and physical appearance (fitness, height, weight, complexion). Certified Peer Recovery Specialists need to learn how to "read" these messages without distorting or over-interpreting them.

3. Listening to and understanding the individual in context.

The Certified Peer Recovery Specialist should listen to the whole person in the context of his or her social settings.

4. Listening with empathy.

Empathetic listening involves attending, observing and listening ("being with") in such a way that the counselor develops an understanding of the peer and his or her world. The Certified Peer Recovery Specialist should put his or her own concerns aside to be fully "with" the person.

Active listening is unfortunately not an easy skill to acquire. Certified Peer Recovery Specialists should be aware of the following hindrances to effective listening:

a) **Inadequate listening:** One can be easily distracted from what other people are talking about if one allows oneself to get lost in one's own thoughts or if one begins to think what to say in reply. Certified Peer Recovery Specialists can often be distracted because they have problems of their own, feel ill, or because they become distracted by social and cultural differences between themselves and their peers. All these factors make it difficult to listen to and understand their peers.

b) **Evaluative listening:** Often, people listen to evaluate others. This means that they are judging and labeling what the other person is saying as either right or wrong, good or bad, acceptable or unacceptable, relevant or irrelevant etc. They then tend to respond evaluatively as well.

c) **Filtered listening:** We tend to listen to ourselves, other people and the world around us through biased filters. Filtered listening distorts our understanding of our peers.

d) **Labels as filters:** Diagnostic labels can hinder one from really listening to their peer. If you see a peer as "that woman with AIDs", your ability to listen empathetically to her problems might be severely distorted and diminished.

e) **Fact-centered rather than person-centered listening:** Asking only informational and factual questions, as opposed to emotional questions, will not solve the peer's problems. Listen to the peer's whole context and focus on themes and core messages.

f) **Rehearsing:** If you mentally rehearse your answers, you are also not listening attentively. Certified Peer Recovery Specialists who listen carefully to the themes and core messages in a person's story always know how to respond. The response may not be a fluent, eloquent or practiced one, but it will at least be appropriate and, more importantly, sincere.

g) **Sympathetic listening:** Although sympathy has its place in human transactions, the use of sympathy is limited in the helping-relationship because it can distort the Certified Peer Support Specialist's listening to the individual's story. To sympathize with someone is to become that person's accomplice. Sympathy conveys pity and even complicity, and pity for the peer can diminish the extent to which you can help the person.

Basic empathy

Basic empathy involves listening, understanding them and their concerns as best as we can, and communicating this understanding back to them in a way that they might understand themselves more fully and act on their understanding. In so doing, empathy is not secrecy, but it builds relationships of trust. It is important to understand that the HIPAA laws encourage empathy because they help set the boundaries of safe and protected relationships towards total healing.

Listening with empathy means that the Certified Peer Recovery Specialist must temporarily forget about his or her own frame of reference. Instead, they must try to see the individual's world and the way they see him or herself as though he or she were seeing it through the eyes of the individual.

Empathy is essentially the ability to recognize and acknowledge the feelings of another person without necessarily experiencing those same emotions. It is an attempt to understand the world of the peer by theoretically stepping into his or her shoes. This understanding of their world must then be shared with them in either a verbal or non-verbal way.

Some of the stumbling blocks to effective empathy are avoiding distracting questions and topics. Certified Peer Recovery Specialists often ask questions to get more information from the peer in order to pursue their own agendas. They might do this at the expense of the individual, and they ignore the feelings that they expressed about his or her experiences. Avoid saying "I know how you feel," because you might not. It can lead to a peer feeling as though you assume you understand their problem, maybe even better than they understand their own problems. That might cause a reluctance for the peer to open up, since it was implied you already know their situation better than they might. No one wants to open up to a know-it-all.

Empathy is not interpreting. The Certified Peer Recovery Specialist should respond to the individual's feelings and should not distort the content of what they are telling you. Although giving advice has its place in peer specialist support, it should be used sparingly. It is crucial to honor the value of self-responsibility.

Empathy is not the same as sympathy. To sympathize with an individual is to show pity, condolence and compassion - all well-intentioned traits but not very helpful in peer advocacy. It is best to always avoid confrontation and arguments with the individual.

Probing or Questioning

Probing involves statements and questions from the Certified Peer Recovery Specialist that enable peers to fully explore any relevant issue within their lives. Probes can take the form of statements, questions, requests, single word or phrases and non-verbal prompts.

Probes or questions serve the following purposes:

- They help encourage non-assertive or reluctant individuals to tell their stories
- They help peers remain focused on relevant and important issues
- They help the peer identify experiences, behaviors and feelings that give a bigger picture of their story. In other words, to fill in missing pieces of the picture
- They can help them move forward in the healing process
- They can also help individuals fully understand themselves and their problem situations

Keep the following in mind when you use probes or questions:

- Try to use questions with caution
- Avoid asking too many questions – you do not want the peer to feel interrogated, and questions often serve as fillers when Certified Peer Recovery Specialists do not know what else to do
- Do not ask a question if you do not want to know the answer
- If you ask two questions in a row, it is probably one question too many
- Although close-ended questions have their place, avoid asking too many close-ended questions that begin with "does", "did", or "is"
- Ask open-ended questions - that is, questions that require more than a simple yes or no answer. Start sentences with: "how", "tell me about", or "what". Open-ended questions are non-threatening, and they encourage description

Summarizing

Sometimes, it is useful for the Certified Peer Recovery Specialist to summarize what was said in a session so as to provide a focus on what was previously discussed and to challenge the individual to move forward. Summaries are particularly helpful under the following circumstances:

- **At the beginning of a new session.** At this point, a summary can give direction to individuals who do not know where to start; it can also prevent individuals from merely repeating what they have already said, and it can gently pressure them to move forward.
- **When a session seems to be going nowhere.** In such circumstances, a summary may help to focus the peer.
- **When an individual does not know what to say next.** In such a situation, a summary may help to move them forward so that he or she can investigate other parts of his or her story.

Integrating communication skills

Skilled Certified Peer Recovery Specialists continually to naturally attend and listen, and use a mix of empathy and probes, to help the peer to come to grips with their issues. Which communication skills will be used and how they will be used depends on the individual, their needs, and the problem or situation.

Writing to the Needs of the Audience

Professional Writing versus Personal Writing

Professional Writing should be implemented when your email, case note, treatment plan, etc. is not for private use. For example, a case note, or treatment plan might be saved in an agency-wide database. If you are working in a hospital setting, any other hospital-based peer, doctor, nurse or social worker will review and utilize your note to further a Peer's treatment goals. Professional writing should always be clear, concise, objective and self-edited.

Professional Communication

The type of language differentiates professional writing from personal writing. For example, professional writing does not use colloquialisms or contractions. In a professional email, one should not use the recipient's first name or informal greeting such as "Hi" or "Hey". Common salutations are Mr., Ms., or

Dr., followed by the recipient's last name. The body paragraph of a professional email should be concise and to the point. Common closings of an email are "Thank you", "Best regards", and "Sincerely".

Name other formal greetings commonly used in professional emails:

_____
_____
_____
_____

Name other formal closing remarks commonly used in professional emails:

_____
_____
_____
_____

Code-Switching

Personal writing allows use of informal language. This writing style is used when communicating with friends or family outside of work. Changing the type of language used based on your audience is known as code-switching. For example, one may use slang when talking to their friends but not with their co-workers.

Name an example of a time where a Peer would use code-switching?

_____
_____
_____
_____
_____

Can you think of a time where you use code-switching language, either in a professional or personal setting?

_____

_____

_____

_____

_____

Reading Independently

Reading Comprehension Issues

Do you ever feel overwhelmed with the amount of reading you have? Do you ever have trouble remaining focused and motivated while reading? Do you ever experience difficulty understanding or remembering what you read? These are common issues that many people face when it comes to reading. With some effective strategies, you can make your reading time meaningful, focused, productive and important. These strategies will prepare peers for rigorous reading and learning.

Active reading

Studies show that you retain more knowledge when you actively engage and interact with texts, rather than reading and re-reading without a clear purpose. Many students practice the type of reading that involves copying down pages of notes word-for-word from the text, creating an outline or simply scanning over pages without really reading them or retaining information. However, these methods do not engage your brain in a way that elicits deep understanding and retention. Active reading forces you to engage with the text.

Before reading

Engaging with a text before reading can crucially boost your understanding and retention. Below are some active reading strategies to use before you read:

- Know Your Purpose

Each text has a purpose that it wants to explain and express. Know what you will be asked to do with the information that you gathered from the reading assignment. Often, reading in preparation for a multiple-choice exam requires a greater attention to detail (such as keywords, definitions, dates, specific concepts and examples) than reading to prepare for discussion or to write an essay (think main points, relationships, tone, setting, use of dialog). Understand your purpose for reading and know what you need to be able to understand. Remember to keep this purpose in mind as you consume a text.

- Integrate Prior Knowledge

Before previewing the text, determine what you already know about the material you are to read. Make text-to-self, text-to-text, and text-to-world connections as text-to-self connections allow students to connect with the text on a personal level. Text-to-text connections are when students are reminded of other texts while they are reading. Text-to-world connections allow students to apply what they are reading to the real world.

- Preview the Text

Give the text an initial glance and note headings, diagrams, tables, pictures, definitions, summaries, and key questions. Reading introductions and conclusions can be helpful truly understand gathering the main idea of the text. After you preview, predict what the section or chapter will be about and what the main concepts are going to be.

While Reading

Keeping your brain active and engaged while you read decreases distractions and confusion. Try some of these strategies to keep yourself focused on the text and engaged in critical thinking.

- **Self-Monitor**

You are the only one who can assure your engagement while reading. It can be very easy for our minds to wander elsewhere. As soon as you notice your mind drifting, stop and consider your needs. Do you need a break? Are you hungry or thirsty? Would a brief walk benefit you? Do you need a more active way to engage with the text? Do you need background noise or movement, or less noise and movement? Do you need to hear the text aloud? What about a change of environment? It is okay to take a break. Before resuming, summarize the last chunk of text you remember to make sure that you know the appropriate starting point.

- **Annotate**

Sometimes one might get carried away with the highlighter. If you feel like you might be doing that and want to try something else, try annotation. Develop a key or a system to note key ideas and major points, unfamiliar words or unclear information, key words and phrases, important information, and connections in the text. Find a method that works for you.

- **Summarize**

After perusing sections of texts (it can be a couple of paragraphs, a page, or even a chunk of text), summarize the main points, plus two or three key details. Put them into your own words. These summaries can serve as the base for your notes while reading.

- **Ask Difficult Questions**

Think like a professor and ask yourself higher level, critical thinking questions, such as:

- What differences exist between _____ and _____?
- How is _____ an example of _____?
- What evidence can you present for _____ and _____?
- What are the specific features of _____?
- What would you predict, based on_____?
- What solutions would you suggest for _____?
- Do you agree that _____? Explain.
- What is the most important feature of _____?
- What is the least important feature of_____?

Reading a text should not end at just the completion of the chapter. Usage of effective after-reading strategies can help you better understand and remember the text for the long-term.

- **Show What You Know**

  - Create an outline of the text from memory, starting with the main points and working toward details. Leave gaps when necessary. You can go back to the text for details or other factors that did not come to mind
  - Discuss the material with a friend, classmate or teacher
  - Teach a family member or friend your new knowledge
  - Brain dump: Give yourself a time limit (such as a few minutes) to write down as much as you remembered
  - Ask yourself questions about the text
  - Identify the important concepts from the reading. Find and provide examples (and non-examples) of each concept.
  - Create a concept map from memory to illustrate your learning from the assigned reading.

- **Investigate further**

  If you have a problem with understanding the reading, locate other resources related to the topic. These resources include a trusted video source, other writing by the same author or web-based study guide. If you still have questions you cannot answer on your own you can always make note of them to ask a professor, TA, or classmate.

- **Self-Test**

  - Make and use flash cards, or possibly a quiz or an outline, to test yourself on what you read. See how much you remember and how much you can explain correctly.
  - Do not peek at the answers or explanations until after you have already answered or explained in your own words.
  - Self-testing in this way will help you think through the information and recall it better in the future.

A purpose of persuasion is to alter another person's ideas or behavior towards a different direction. These techniques are commonly used in effective persuasion.

Establish a Common Ground

Building a rapport with your peer is one of the best ways to effectively use persuasion techniques. People naturally trust others when they see themselves having a commonality or likeness. It is essential to find some commonality with your peer in order to build a proper relationship. Ask questions and be genuinely attentive, smile, be confident, enthusiastic and respectful.

Point Out the Benefits

As a peer, you should highlight the benefits of recovery. Using personal experiences, show how it is a positive change by aligning with their personal goals. Avoid pushing an agenda on to the peer, but instead create a picture of sobriety that highlights that benefits as it applies personally to the individual. Guide your peer in a direction that will benefit them.

Turn Objections into Strengths

Doubt and opposition are common. A clear understanding of your role will help you to counter any objections and criticism raised. You should agree with the peer's objection and then illustrate how to overcome that obstacle. Illustrate the advantages that will eliminate the peer's pain points and help satisfy their wants.

Commitment and Consistency

Find a small goal for the peer to accomplish. Once committed, the peer will most likely agree to a larger goal later. This technique employs the fact that people tend to behave in a consistent manner. Once a small goal is mastered, the larger goals seem possible. If your peer is struggling, reaching one small goal a day can result in an amazing, positive impact.

Use the Reciprocity Principle

The principle states that when someone does something for us, we feel obligated to return the favor.

Social Proof Technique

Social proof is the idea that people tend to follow a presented idea when they do not have sufficient information to make the decision on their own. This technique is most often used in celebrity endorsements or customer testimonials.

Scarcity

This involves letting people know that they stand to lose. In sales, it refers to attempting a quick sale by reiterating a deadline or quantity limits.

Assertiveness

To be assertive means being direct about what you need, want, feel or believe in a way that's respectful of the views of others. It is a communication skill that can reduce conflict, build your self-confidence and improve relationships in the workplace.

Here are some tips to help you learn to be more assertive:

1. **Decide to positively assert yourself.** Commit to being assertive rather than passive or aggressive and start practicing today.

2. **Retrieve open and honest communication.** Remember to respect other people when you are sharing your feelings, wants, needs, beliefs or opinions.

3. **Listen actively.** Try to understand the other person's point of view and do not interrupt when they are explaining it to you.

4. **Agree to disagree.** Remember that having a different point of view does not mean you are right, and the other person is wrong. It is okay to disagree and it does not have to be negative.

5. **Avoid guilt trips.** Be honest and tell others how you feel or what you want without making accusations or making them feel guilty.

6. **Stay calm.** Breathe normally, look the person in the eye, keep your face relaxed and speak in a normal voice.

7. **Take a problem-solving approach to conflict.** Try to see the other person as your friend, not your enemy.

8. **Practice assertiveness.** Talk in a forthcoming way in front of a mirror or with a friend. Pay attention to your body language as well as to the words you say.

9. **Use 'I'.** Stick with statements that include 'I' in them such as 'I think' or 'I feel'. Don't use accusatory language such as 'you always' or 'you never'.

10. **Be patient.** Being assertive is a skill that needs practice. Remember that you will sometimes do better at it than at other times, but you can always learn from your mistakes.

Writing SOAP Notes

SOAP notes are a style of documentation commonly used by Peer Recovery Specialists to write notes about a peer. SOAP notes are most commonly used in hospital and clinical-based settings. The acronym SOAP stands for subjective, objective, assessment, and plan. The subjective portion contains a summary statement by the Peer Recovery Specialist, which can include how the peer is feeling, along with any medical history or family history. The objective portion contains medical information that follows the subjective statement. This is usually something the Peer Recovery Specialist completes during a peer interaction. The assessment portion contains information that the Peer Recovery Specialist pieces together based on the interaction (identifying the issue). Finally, the plan portion states the plan for future clinical work.

Subjective data: What the peer tells us about their experience

Example 1: peer describes feeling very tired in the morning and not being able to get out of bed until 11:00am after starting new medication. It is impacting ability to participate in therapy. Worried about progress in recovery.

Example 2: Peer reports great concern about losing housing – owner is losing the property. Peer reports not sleeping well, lack of appetite and does not know what he is going to do.

Objective: What you observe or find during peer session

Example 1: Peer yawning during noon appointment, appears less kept than usual, and speech is slow and clipped.

Example 2: Peer is visibly upset – crying, frantic speech, pacing, often shifting in seat

Assessment: The Peer Recovery Specialist's opinion or interpretation of the Peer's situation as reported and you observe. The conclusions made in the assessment are more than a restatement of the problem, as it determines whether or not the situation can be resolved.

Example 1: Appears that Peer is having difficulty with new medication. Peer committed to finding a different way to manage the difficulty.

Example 2: Peer upset about possible loss of housing and its effects on Peer's health

Plan: What do the Peer and the case manager want to do to resolve the situation?

ACTIVITY: You are a Peer Recovery Specialist in a hospital emergency room. You are assigned to work with a Peer who was admitted last night after an accidental overdose. You are tasked with conducting an initial interaction in order to gather information for the Peer's recovery plan. Using SOAP notes formatting, document your meeting.
Write out a set of SOAP notes on that peer.

S_____

_____
_____
_____

O_____

_____
_____
_____

A_____

_____
_____
_____

P_____

_____
_____

_____

Check for Understanding

1. How has the presence of Social Media affected Professional and Workplace Etiquette?
2. Name 5 Dos and 5 Don'ts of Workplace Etiquette
3. Define Person-Centered Language and give an example.
4. What does SOLER stand for?
5. What does SOAP stand for?

Further Application

Pair up with a partner and conduct an interview using SOLER techniques. Present to the class using examples of what to do AND what not to do as both an interviewer and interviewee.

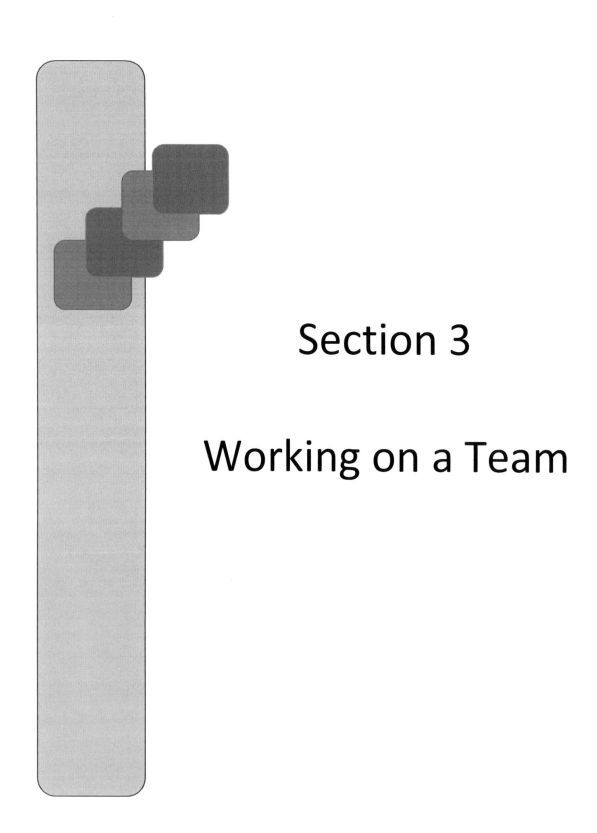

Section 3

Working on a Team

Team-Building Icebreaker Idea

1. Divide into groups of three to five people (based on the number of people in the class)

2. Everyone must find ten things that they have in common with every other person in the group. The commonalities must have nothing to do with work, body parts or clothing.

3. One person must take notes and be ready to read the group's list of ten commonalities to the whole group upon completion of the assignment.

4. Compare each group's list of items with the lists generated in the other small groups.

Age diversity in the workplace

Peer Recovery Specialists span across a wide range of ages. The same is true for the peers experiencing recovery. In today's job market, employers are looking for both mature and experienced professionals, as well as younger, entry-level employees. A successful employer embraces age diversity in the workplace. Why? Here are a few examples. For each example, describe how it relates to a Peer Recovery Specialist.

- Encouraging creativity and innovation

_____
_____
_____
_____

- Understanding customers, clients, peers

_____
_____
_____
_____

- Boosting your employer brand

_____
_____
_____
_____

- Mentoring one another

_____
_____
_____
_____

- Beginning to bridge the growing digital skills gap

_____

_____

_____

_____

- Creating a great company culture by giving all employees a voice

_____

_____

_____

_____

Teamwork

When people are encouraged to work as a team, a sense of comradery is typically naturally strengthened. Teamwork is always a helpful tool in a range of situations within a professional work environment. Employees can utilize team building skills, crisis management, problem-solving or even social planning.

How would each of these situations relate to teamwork in a Peer Recovery Specialist setting?

1.Respect and Trust

_____

_____

_____

2.Open Communication

_____

_____

_____

3.Diversity of Capabilities

4.Clearly Outline Roles and Responsibilities

_____

_____

_____

5.Encourage Creative Freedom

_____

_____

_____

Boundaries and Working Within Them

A Role Boundary is a clear definition of the duties, rights and limitations of facilitators, volunteers and program participants. Recovery support services, as the term is used here, refers to non-clinical services that are designed to help initiate and sustain individual/family recovery from severe alcohol and other drug problems and to enhance the quality of individual/family recovery.

The Center for Substance Abuse Treatment's Recovery Community Support Program identified four types of recovery support services:

1. **Emotional support** - demonstrations of empathy, love, caring, and concern in such activities as peer mentoring and recovery coaching, as well as recovery support groups.
2. **Informational support** - provision of health and wellness information, educational assistance, and help in acquiring new skills, ranging from life skills to employment readiness and citizenship restoration.
3. **Instrumental support** - concrete assistance in task accomplishment, especially with stressful or unpleasant tasks such as filling out applications and obtaining entitlements, providing child care, transportation to support-group meetings, and clothing closets.
4. **Companionship** - helping people in early recovery feel connected and enjoy

being with others, especially in recreational activities in alcohol- and drug-free environments. This assistance is especially needed in early recovery, when little about abstaining from alcohol or drugs is reinforcing and relapse is common.

Some of the service activities now provided within the rubric of recovery support services include activities performed in earlier decades by persons working as outreach workers, case managers, counselor assistants, and volunteers. Recovery support services may be provided by clinically-trained professionals as an adjunct to their clinical (assessment and counseling) activities, or they may be delivered by persons in recovery who are not clinically trained, but who are trained and supervised to provide such support services. They are being provided as adjuncts to other service roles or as a specialty role. They are being provided by persons working in full and part-time paid roles and by persons who provide these services as volunteers.

Peer-based recovery support roles are growing rapidly in the mental health and addiction service arenas. While there are specific issues related to peer-based services that are distinct within these fields, all of the fields have much they can learn from each other. Part of what makes the ethical delivery of recovery support services so challenging in the addictions context is that the Certified Peer Recovery Specialist performs many roles.

In service organizations, a Certified Peer Recovery Specialist is described as a(n):

Outreach Worker - Identifies and engages hard-to-reach individuals; offers living proof of transformative power of recovery; makes recovery attractive

Motivator and Cheerleader - Exhibits faith in capacity for change; encourages and celebrates recovery achievements; mobilizes internal and external recovery resources; encourages self-advocacy and economic self-sufficiency

Ally and Confidant - Genuinely cares and listens; can be trusted with confidence

Truth-teller - Provides feedback on recovery progress

Role model and Mentor - Offers his/her life as living proof of the transformative power of recovery; provides stage-appropriate recovery education

Planner - Facilitates the transition from a professional-directed treatment plan to consumer-developed and consumer-directed personal recovery plan

Problem Solver - Helps resolve personal and environmental obstacles to recovery resource broker (links individuals/families to formal and indigenous sources of sober housing, recovery-conducive employment, health and social services, and recovery support; matches individuals to particular support groups/ meetings)

Monitor- Processes each peer's response to professional services and mutual aid exposure to enhance service/support engagement, reduce attrition, resolve problems in the service/support relationship, and facilitate development of a long-term, sobriety-based support network; provides periodic face-to-face, telephonic or email-based monitoring of recovery stability and, when needed, provides early re-intervention and recovery re-initiation services

Tour Guide - Introduces newcomers into the local culture of recovery; provides an orientation to recovery roles, rules, rituals, language, and etiquette; opens opportunities for broader community participation

Support Specialist - Helps individuals and families navigate complex service systems

Educator - Provides each peer with normative information about the stages of recovery; informs professional helpers, the community, and potential service consumers about the prevalence, pathways, and styles of long-term recovery

Community Organizer- Helps develop and expand available recovery support resources; enhances cooperative relationships between professional service organizations and indigenous recovery support groups; cultivates opportunities for people in recovery to participate in volunteerism and other acts of service to the community

Lifestyle Consultant/Guide - Assists individuals/families to develop sobriety-based rituals of daily living; encourages activities (across religious, spiritual, and secular) frameworks that enhance life meaning and purpose

Friend - Provides sober companionship; a social bridge from the culture of addiction to the culture of recovery

Role Boundary Integrity:

The Certified Peer Recovery Specialist is NOT a:	You are moving beyond the boundaries of the Certified Peer Recovery Specialist role if you:
Sponsor (or equivalent)	<ul><li>Perform AA/NA or other mutual aid group service work in your RC role</li><li>Guide someone through the steps or principles of a particular recovery program</li></ul>
Therapist/counselor	<ul><li>Diagnose</li><li>Provide counseling or refer to your support activities as "counseling" or "therapy"</li><li>Focus on problems/trauma as opposed to recovery solutions</li></ul>
Nurse/Physician	<ul><li>Suggest or express disagreement with medical diagnoses</li><li>Offer medical advice</li><li>Make statements about prescribed drugs beyond the boundaries of your training and experience</li></ul>
Priest/Clergy	<ul><li>Promote a particular religion/church</li><li>Interpret religious doctrine</li><li>Offer absolution / forgiveness</li><li>Provide pastoral counseling</li></ul>

Working independently allows an individual to work at their own pace, while working as part of a team increases collaboration and allows brainstorming.

Using the diagram below, list the positive aspects of working as an Individual vs Working as a Member of a Team in the Peer Recovery Workforce.

Individual Work   **Teamwork**

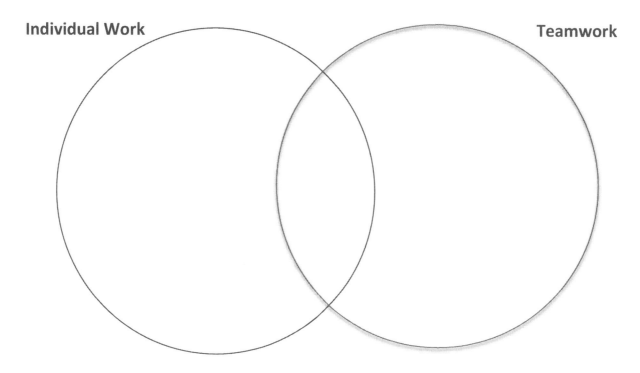

Identifying Strengths

When working with a team, you must always understand that each person has different strengths and weaknesses. It is important to have an open and non-judgmental view to leverage each other's strengths and make the best impact for the peers you are there to support

This does not mean letting weakness you have go underdeveloped. Learn from your co-workers and help others learn from you. You should play up your strengths while addressing any weaknesses. The same applies to the strengths and weaknesses of your team

An effective and continuous feedback program creates a culture of constructive communication

Also examine your weaknesses. How can you improve them? What actions could you take to reduce any associated risks? What types of supports can you request from your supervisor to assist with developing skills in these areas?

List your personal strengths and weaknesses. How could the support of a supervisor in the workplace help to mold these into successful characteristics as a Peer?

STRENGTHS	WEAKNESSES

Enhancement of coaching and mentoring skills in the workplace will improve your later skills while working with peers. It is important to listen, empathize and encourage. When giving feedback to peers, it should be constructive, motivating, specific and actionable. The underlying feeling should always be that of respect.

What are some examples of respectful and constructive feedback that a Peer could utilize in the workplace?

_____

_____

_____

_____

_____

_____

_____

_____

_____

_____

CONFLICT RESOLUTION

Conflict is often natural and often unavoidable when working with others. This is because of differences in work goals and personal styles. Follow these guidelines for handling conflict in the workplace.

1. Talk with the other person.

  • Ask the other person to name a time when it would be convenient to meet

  • Meet in a place where you will not be interrupted.

2. Focus on behavior and events, not on personalities.

  • Say "When this happens …" instead of "When you do …"

  • Describe a specific instance or event instead of generalizing

3. Listen carefully.

  • Listen to what the other person is saying instead of focusing on your reaction

  • Avoid interruption

  • After the other person finishes speaking, rephrase what was said to make sure you understand it

  • Ask questions to clarify your understanding

4. Identify points of agreement and disagreement.

  • Summarize the areas of agreement and disagreement

  • Ask the other person if he or she agrees with your assessment

  • Modify your assessment until both of you agree on the areas of conflict

5. Prioritize the areas of conflict.

  • Discuss which areas of conflict are most important to each of you to resolve

6. Develop a plan to work on each conflict.

  • Always start with the most important conflict

  • Focus on the future

  • Set up future meeting times to continue your discussions

7. Follow through on your plan.

>• Keep with the discussions until you've worked through each area of conflict

>• Maintain a collaborative attitude

8. Build on your success.

>• Look for opportunities to point out progress

>• Compliment the other person's insights and achievements

>• Congratulate each other when you make progress, even if it's just a small step. Your hard work will pay off when scheduled discussions eventually give way to ongoing, friendly communication

Check for Understanding

1. Name and describe the 4 types of recovery Support Services.
2. What is meant by Role Boundary Integrity?
3. What are the 8 guidelines for conflict resolution in a professional setting?

Further Application

1. Based on the list, "Certified Peer Recovery Specialists are described as..." find the three that best describe your strengths and the three that most match your weaknesses. How can you utilize these strengths and improve upon your weaknesses to make you a stronger candidate in the Peer Recovery Workforce?

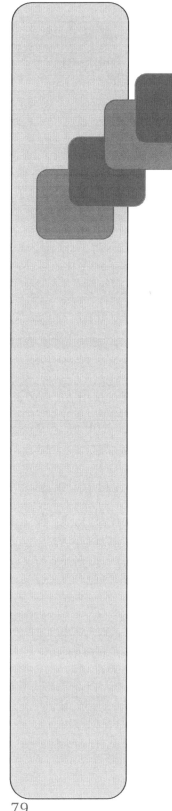

Section 4

Problem Solving

In order to support individuals with the development of problem-solving skills, you must become familiar with common problem-solving skills. Review and practice the skills listed below. Once you are comfortable, practice them with individuals to support the development of conflict resolution skills. Make up scenarios and situations where you have the ability to practice the skills listed below.

1. Focus on the solution – not the problem
It can be hard, but you need to try not to overthink the problem. Neuroscientists have proven that your brain cannot find solutions if you focus on the problem. This is because when you focus on the problem you are effectively feeding negativity, which in turn activates negative emotions in the brain. These emotions block potential solutions. It helps to first acknowledge the problem and then move your focus to a solution-oriented mindset where you keep fixed on what the answer could be instead of lingering on what went wrong and whose fault it is.

2. Have an open mind
Try and entertain all solutions, even if they seem ridiculous at first. It is important you keep an open mind and boost creative thinking. This can trigger potential solutions. In the corporate advertising industry it is drummed into you that 'No idea is a bad idea' and this aids creative thinking in brainstorms and other problem-solving techniques. Even if the solution is more complex, it is often a collaborative effort between the Certified Peer Support Specialist, other members of the support team, and the peer being supported. Whatever you do, do not ridicule yourself for coming up with what you might consider stupid solutions. Often, it is the crazy ideas that trigger other more viable solutions.

3. View problems neutrally
Try not to view problems as scary things. They are what you make of them. A problem is really just a form of feedback on your current situation. All a problem is telling you is that something is not currently working and that you need to find a new way around it. Try and approach problems neutrally and without any judgment. If you get caught up in the problem this may trigger a lot of negative thoughts and block any potential solutions.

4. Think laterally

Change the direction of your thoughts by thinking laterally. Try to change your approach and look at things in a new way. You can try flipping your objective around and looking for a solution that is the complete opposite. Even if it feels silly, a fresh and unique approach usually stimulates a fresh solution.

5. Use language that creates possibility

Lead your thinking with phrases like 'what if...' and 'imagine if...' Improv often teaches people the phrase, "Yes, and..." to always keep building on ideas. These terms open up our brains to think creatively and encourage solutions. Avoid closed, negative language such as 'I don't think...' or 'This is not right but...'.

6. Simplify things

As human beings we have a tendency to make things more complicated than they need to be! Try simplifying your problem by generalizing it. Remove all the detail and go back to the basics. Try looking for a really easy, obvious solution – you might be surprised at the results! We all know that it's often the simple things that are the most productive.

Independence and Initiative

Demonstrating independence in problem solving often means you can work through the problem without guidance. Taking initiative when it comes to problem-solving means that you act without being asked. Try to remember it is not a problem, it is an opportunity for improvement and growth. For example, a peer is worried about losing their housing. There is no need to dwell on the unfortunate situation. Brainstorm options, such as moving in with a friend or family member, looking into state or federally funded options, or speaking to the landlord to make a new arrangement. Stay neutral and remember that while it is a home, it is replaceable. It does not have to be scary when you remember that this could potentially lead to something better. Remember that something positive can easily come from this experience. Stay mindful about the fact that we all relocate and, while it is inconvenient at times, it is doable.

Can you think of a time where you demonstrated independence and initiative when problem-solving either personally or professionally?

_____
_____
_____
_____
_____
_____
_____

Problem Solving and Critical Thinking

Step 1: Identify the problem. Break it down into smaller steps and decide what action to take first.
Step 2: Brainstorm and write down as many ideas as you can that might help solve the problem, no matter how silly they seem – don't dismiss any possible solutions.

Step 3: Consider the pros and cons of each possible solution.

Step 4: Choose one of the possible solutions that looks likely to work, based on the advantages and disadvantages.

Step 5: Plan out step-by-step what you need to do to carry out this solution. What? When? How? With whom or what? What could cause problems? How can you get around those problems? Is this realistic and achievable?

Step 6: Do it! Carry out the plan.

Step 7: Review how it went. Was it helpful? Did you achieve what you set out to achieve? If not, how could you have done it differently? Did you achieve any progress, however small, towards your goal? What have you learned?

Step 8: If you achieved your goal – consider tackling the next step of your original problem. If you didn't fully achieve your goal – adjust your chosen solution or return to steps 3 and 4 and choose another possible solution.

Things to Consider When Advocating for the Recovery Needs of Peers

1. Be respectful

It is important to be respectful to the individual as their advocate. It is equally important when advocating for them to be respectful to others as well. Deciding how to point out where priorities should lie should involve thoughtfulness, wisdom, compassion, and respect for other people.

2. Respect time

When you meet with any type of decision-maker or someone providing services for individuals you are advocating for, their time is often spread very thin. Arrive prepared and respect the time frame that you have. This will increase your chances of more frequent and positive interactions with these individuals in the future.

3. Stay on task

If you get distracted from your goal, so will whoever is listening to you. When talking to someone about the issues, stay focused on your cause and topic at hand. Writing out a goal or mission with objectives and action steps to complete those goals can help you stay focused on what best promotes your cause.

4. Respect the individual's point of view

Be open to other points of view. The individual you are advocating for needs to be acknowledged and allowed to contribute their thoughts and opinions as well as who you are speaking to when advocating for a peer.

5. Respect yourself as well

Acknowledge that when you know an issue, you know it. If you completed significant work on a topic and trust the research you've done, say so. Present that research when advocating for the peer.

6. Get comfortable

Research a variety of ways to advocate and practice those skills. Writing petitions, submitting testimony, in-person meetings, phone calls, etc. are all methods of advocacy.

Petition Activity

As a group, find a topic within the recovery scope where you believe advocacy is needed for advancements. Fill in the petition template below to make your point.

(Date)

Dear _____,

 (name your audience)

We are _____

 (name yourself, group or organization)

We want to _____

 (describe your issue)

_____

_____

We feel this would benefit us by _____

 (give supporting reasons)

_____

_____

_____

_____

_____

_____

We, the undersigned, call on _____

(restate your audience)

to make a difference by _____

 (state call to action)

_____

_____

_____

Signed by:

_____   _____

_____   _____

_____   _____

SWOT Analysis and Other Problem-Solving Tools

A SWOT analysis is a tool to help you develop your professional goals and identify possible strengths and weaknesses.

SWOT stands for Strengths, Weaknesses, Opportunities, and Threats.

Strengths and weaknesses are internal. They are things that you have some control over and can change. Examples of these include your team members, peers, intellectual property, location.

Opportunities and threats are external. They are things that are going on outside your organization. You can take advantage of opportunities and protect against threats, but you cannot change them. Examples include competitors, budget, confidentiality issues, staffing.

A SWOT analysis organizes your top strengths, weaknesses, opportunities, and threats into an organized list and is usually presented in a simple two-by-two grid.

Strengths

- What advantages does your organization have?

- What do you do better than anyone else?

Weaknesses

- What could you improve?

- What should you avoid?

Opportunities

- What good opportunities can you spot?

- What interesting trends are you aware of?

Useful opportunities can come from such things as:

- Changes in technology and markets on both a broad and narrow scale.

- Changes in government policy related to your field.

- Changes in social patterns, population profiles, lifestyle changes, and so on.

- Local events.

Threats

- What obstacles do you face?

- Is changing technology threatening your position?

- Do you have budgeting concerns?

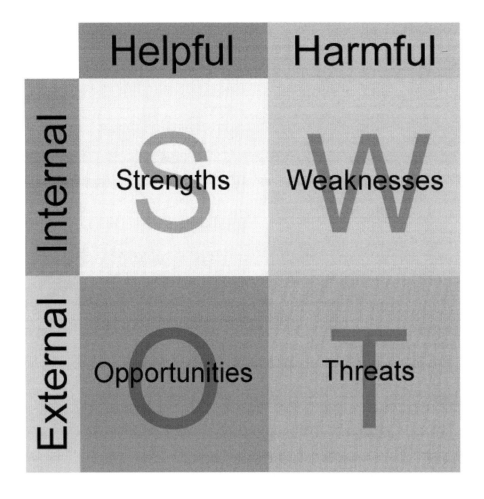

Check for Understanding

1. What does it mean to think laterally?
2. What does it mean to view problems neutrally?
3. What 6 things should you consider when advocating for the recovery needs of peers?
4. What does SWOT stand for?

Further Application

2. Using the SWOT template, complete the table for a professional concern that you need to solve.

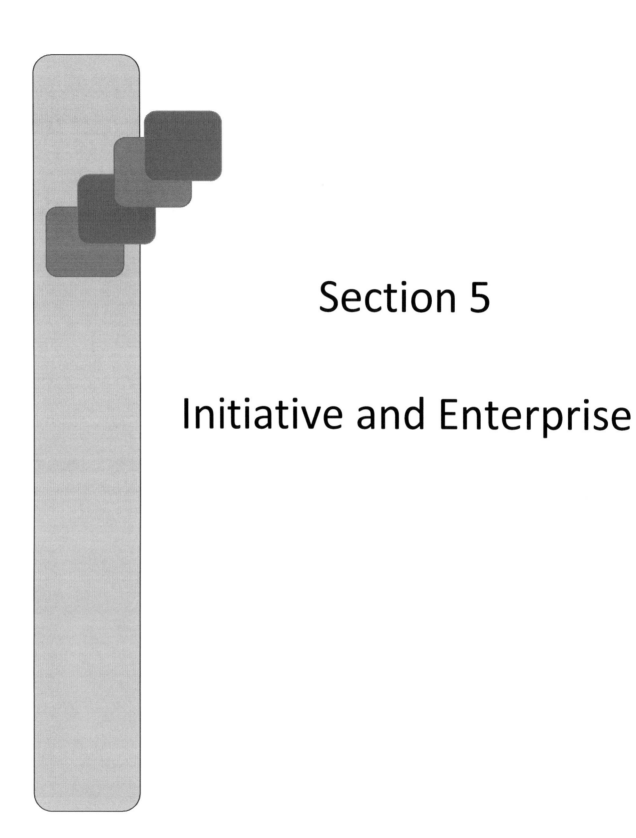

Section 5

Initiative and Enterprise

Problem-Solving Activity

Work through the steps listed below to solve one of the presenting problems:

Presenting Problem #1: The Peer Recovery Specialists at your Recovery House are not properly trained in continuous education, including community safety measures, motivational interviewing and trauma-informed care. Your annual budget does not allow for traditional training methods, but your Peer Recovery Specialists must maintain their education hours in order to fulfill the requirements of their certification.

Presenting Problem #2: A peer relapsed and is in the emergency room. You feel defeated and are questioning your ability as a Certified Peer Recovery Specialist. Your peer's sponsor called you and asked you to meet him at the hospital to talk your peer through his relapse.

Presenting Problem #3: You are employed as a Certified Peer Recovery Specialist in a local hospital. Without notice, your shift hours were changed from daytime to overnight hours. You are a single parent and cannot work the newly assigned hours.

Step 1: Prepare yourself for change rather than ignoring it
Anticipate potential changes or uncertainty with a work or team project and list your concerns. When anticipating change, talk through your concerns with a third party who is not as invested in the situation. Their perspective should help you pick up what you are missing rather than avoiding it. With whom would you discuss your concerns?

_____

_____

_____

_____

_____

_____

Step 2: Work on being flexible in the face of change

When change happens, admit to yourself that you cannot change the reality that things are now different. The only thing you have control over is how you react to new circumstances.

_____

_____

_____

_____

_____

Step 3: Decide what you can do to make the uninvited changes in your work life produce what you want

Make a list of potential positive outcomes that still exist despite the change. Use this list to keep you motivated as you work to achieve your goals.

_____

_____

_____

_____

_____

_____

_____

Further Application

Identify a problem in your personal or professional life and problem-solve the issue using the list of steps from the activity.

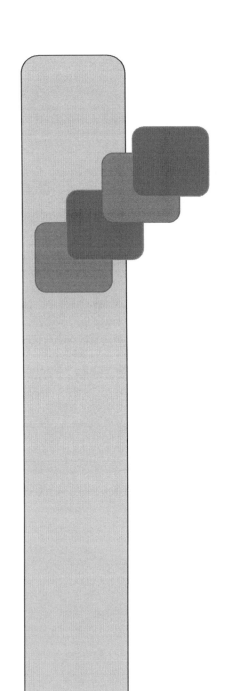

Section 6

Self-Management

Personal Vision and Goals

A personal vision can describe how you commit to living your life. A personal vision can be generated by both short-term goals and long-term goals. Goal-setting is a helpful tool used to move you toward your vision. Most individuals have a personal vision centering around career aspirations and family structure.

We might be here for a specific purpose but what helps us move and direct our purpose is a vision or a goal. Vision gives direction, as well as a glimpse over our life, to make our goals and purpose become a reality. In order to understand where we want ourselves to be in life, we must have a clear vision of a goal in our life. So, once you understand that vision clarifies purpose, life will become simpler and more meaningful.

Turning Ideas Into Action

Setting SMART Goals

There are many variations of what SMART stands for, but the essence is this – goals should be:
Specific
Measurable
Attainable
Relevant
Time Bound

Set Specific Goals

Your goal must be clear and well defined. Vague or generalized goals are better than nothing, but not as helpful. They do not provide sufficient direction. Remember, you need goals to show you the way. Make it as easy as you can to get where you want to go by defining precisely where you want to end up.

Set Measurable Goals

Include precise places, amounts, dates, and more in your goals so you can measure your degree of success. If your goal is simply defined to reduce expenses, how will you know when you have been successful unless you keep track? Without a way to measure your success you miss out on the celebration that comes with knowing you have actually achieved something.

Set Attainable Goals

Make sure that it is possible to achieve the goals you set. If you set a goal that you have no hope of achieving, you will only demoralize yourself and possibly erode your confidence. That being said, resist the urge to set goals that are too easy. Accomplishing a goal that you did not have to work hard for can be anticlimactic and can make you fear setting future goals that carry a risk of non-achievement. By setting realistic yet challenging goals, you hit the balance you need. These are the types of goals that require you to try hard and they bring the greatest personal satisfaction.

Set Relevant Goals

Goals should be relevant to the direction you want your life and career to take. By keeping goals aligned with this, you'll develop the focus you need to get ahead and do what you want. Set widely scattered and inconsistent goals, and the result might be wasting your time.

Set Time-Bound Goals

Your goals must have a deadline. This means that you know when you can celebrate success. When you are working on a deadline, your sense of urgency increases and achievement will come much quicker. While you are helping individuals set goals make it a practice putting said goals in writing. The physical act of writing down a goal makes it real and tangible. You lack an excuse for forgetting about it. A method that is practical and efficient for those in recovery is the use of a service plan. There are many examples of these and you may see them called other names, but the structure is very similar.

SMART Goal Worksheet

Today's Date: _____ Target Date: _____ Start Date: _____

Date Achieved: _____

Goal:

_____

Verify that your goal is SMART

Specific: What exactly will you accomplish? - You will need to clearly define a goal (s) that resulted from completing the purpose equation. What will you produce?

_____

_____

_____

_____

Measurable: How will you know when you have reached this goal? How will you know when you produced it?

_____

_____

_____

_____

Achievable: Is achieving this goal realistic with effort and commitment? Have you got the resources to achieve this goal (s)? If not, who (people or organizations) or what (money=grants, fundraising, etc., time=babysitter, scheduling, replacing time wasting activities, etc.) will help you get what you need to achieve this goal?

_____

_____

_____

_____

Relevant: Why is this goal significant to your life? Does it connect to your Purpose Equation?

_____
_____
_____
_____

Timely: When will you achieve this goal?

_____
_____
_____
_____

This goal is important because:

_____
_____
_____
_____

The benefits of achieving this goal will be:

_____
_____
_____
_____

Take Action:

Potential Obstacles   Potential Solutions

_____   _____
_____   _____
_____   _____
_____   _____
_____   _____
_____   _____

Who are the people you will ask to help you?

_____

_____

_____

_____

Who will you ask to hold you accountable to produce what you need to produce?

_____

_____

_____

_____

Specific Action Steps: What steps need to be taken to get you to your goal?

What was
Completed?   Expected Completion Date

_____   _____

_____

_____   _____

_____

_____   _____

_____

_____   _____

_____

Evaluating and Monitoring Recovery

As a Peer Recovery Specialist, having insight into your own recovery process is essential. SAMHSA describes the following techniques to strengthen one's own recovery while conducting the work as a Peer. For each technique, describe how you can apply it to your own recovery in both a personal and professional setting.

Accepting that recovery is a lifelong process:

_____

_____

_____

_____

Practice Control over Emotions, Activities, Relationships, Choices:

_____

_____

_____

_____

Detaching from People, Places, Things, Times that trigger addiction:

_____

_____

_____

_____

Reading the Signals and Knowing Your Triggers:

_____

_____

_____

Relaxation Time

_____

_____

_____

_____

Partnership and Communication/Support Groups/Wellness Support

_____

_____

_____

_____

Balance of Work, Sleep, Recovery activities, Relationships, Leisure activities

_____

_____

_____

_____

Addressing underlying issues that may surface

_____

_____

_____

_____

Focus on Nutrition and Exercise

_____

_____

_____

WDEP SYSTEM

The Peer Recovery Specialist using Glasser's choice theory, WDEP system, applies the principles to peers in various organizations. Central to the effective use of the system is the establishment of a fair, firm, and friendly atmosphere, climate, environment, and an encouraging relationship.

Built on the above environment, the procedures using the WDEP system, include:

- **Wants:** Helping peers define and clarify their wants

- **Doing:** Examining their total behavior: feelings, effective or ineffective self-talk, and especially their actions

- **Evaluation:** A searching and even at times uncomfortable self-evaluation

- **Plan:** Culminating in specific and attainable positive plan for improvement

- For ongoing peer services, the Peer Recovery Specialist should interview the peer at the start of peer services, during a midpoint review and before terminating services.
- For short term or brief services, the Peer Recovery Specialist may interview the peer and provide the peer with a written plan the peer can take with them. When possible, the Peer Recovery Specialist should conduct a follow-up within a reasonable amount of time.
- It is important that the peer identify their own goals. The Peer Recovery Specialist can advocate, encourage and share their own success stories within these domains as this may motivate the peer to strengthen goals where there may be apparent gaps.
- It is important to cover all of the domains within the peer interview. However, the interview can be conducted over multiple sessions within a 3-week timeframe.

- Additional domains can be added to the worksheet to ensure any of the peer's individual goals that may fall outside of these domains are reflected.

WDEP: Activity

<u>WDEP Worksheet</u>

Peer Name: _____ DOB: _____
Peer Support Worker's Name: _____
Start Date: _____
Day: _____ Month: _____ Year: _____

1st Review ☐   2nd Review ☐   3rd Review ☐

Domain	Want	Doing	Evaluating	Planning
	What do you want instead of the problem? If you woke up tomorrow and your life would be perfect how would you know it? What would be different? Is this what you want? What do your loved ones desire for you?	What are you doing? (thinking, acting, and feeling) When you are acting this way what are you thinking? When you think this way, how are you feeling?	Is what you are doing, helping you get what you want? Is it taking you in the direction you want to go? Is what you want achievable? Does it help you to look at it in that way?	What are you willing to do/think differently to get what you want? Are you clear about what you want to get? What can you start doing immediately? What types of things are you willing to engage in to help

	What do you want to get out of meeting with me as your Peer?	How do your thoughts, acts and feelings impact your recovery? Health?	How hard are you prepared to work at this? Is your current level of commitment working in your favor? Is it a helpful plan?	you attain what you want? Examples can include: • Professional counseling • Faith based activities • Education • Support Group • Exercising • Seeing a medical doctor, etc.
Relationships (family, friends, spouse)				
Occupational (Career, Educational)				

Medical
Health

Mental Health
(emotional
well-being)

Spirituality (values, meaning, life goals, faith)				
Other				

Resources
List the resources the Peer recovery professional will support the peer with attaining to help the peer achieve their goals.

_____	_____
_____	_____
_____	_____
_____	_____
_____	_____
_____	_____
_____	_____

Peer Signature: _____

Date: _____

Peer recovery professional Signature: _____

Date: _____

Developing Cultural Awareness

Cultural awareness is defined as the ability to understand the differences between yourself and people from other countries, backgrounds, age groups, religions or genders. It is essential in the Peer Recovery Workforce to strengthen the understanding of people who differ from you in order to promote workplace diversity and mutual respect.

The follow list describes techniques for strengthening cultural awareness:

1. **Culture extends beyond skin color.** Although darker-skinned persons are commonly identified as black or African-American, some identify themselves as Hispanic, Jamaican, or white. Others may identify with their religion, gender, sexual preference, age, geography, socioeconomic status, or occupation.

2. **Attempt to find out each peer's cultural background.** On your intake forms, include questions about race, ethnicity, language(s), religion, and

age, or ask the peer to discuss his or her cultural background during the initial interview. These questions should be optional.

3. **Determine your cultural effectiveness.** A sample breakdown of your peers can help you analyze treatment, compliance, progress, and outcomes among cultural groups.

4. **Make your peers feel at home.** If possible, your staff should reflect your area's cultural makeup as much as possible. It will help increase the comfort of peers.

5. **Conduct culturally sensitive evaluations.** Cultural identification often leads to misdiagnosis. For example, African-American men tend to be over-diagnosed with paranoid schizophrenia or antisocial personality disorder.

6. **Elicit peer expectations and preferences.** Some cultures distrust modern drug therapy, while some peers think medication should magically resolve their disorders.

7. **Understand your cultural identity.** Do a cultural self-analysis and see how your values apply to your peers. For example, if your culture values independence and individuality, you may underestimate the effectiveness of family therapy for peers whose cultures value interdependence.

Peer Networks and Professional Development

Credentialing – Jordan Peer Recovery Training is a NAADAC and IC&RC certified training program. JPRT meets the educational requirements for peers to sit for the NAADAC National Certified Peer Recovery Support Specialist (NCPRSS) exam.

NAADAC.ORG describes the benefits of credentialing as a Peer:

National Certified Peer Recovery Support Specialist (NCPRSS)
Peer Recovery Support Specialists are individuals who are in recovery from substance use or co-occurring mental health disorders. Their life experiences and recovery allow them to provide recovery support in such way that others can benefit from their experiences.

The purpose of the experiential-based National Certified Peer Recovery Support Specialist Credential is to standardize the knowledge and responsiveness of peer support to individuals with substance use and co-occurring mental health disorders.

- o Position yourself for career opportunities and reimbursement potential.
- o NCC AP's NCPRSS Certification is endorsed by Optum as a reimbursed credential.
- o Distinguish yourself as a recovering person that evidences responsiveness and knowledge in recovery support services.
- o The NCPRSS credential reflects a commitment of the highest ethical standards for Peer Recovery Support Specialists.

Continuous education

Jordan Peer Recovery Training offers online and in-person courses to maintain NCPRSS certification. Each year, certified Peers must complete 20 hours of continuing education credits. JPRT's specialized trainings allow Peers to maintain their certification, while simultaneously focusing on a concentration such as Veteran-based services, Peers on College Campuses, Forensic-Based Peer Recovery, Peer Recovery for Youth and Adolescents, and more.

- o Jordan Peer Recovery Training online courses can be found at jordanpeerrecovery.thinkific.com

RESOURCE USAGE

TIME MANAGEMENT (SCHEDULING-RESCHEDULING PEERS RECEIVING SERVICES)

Specific Scheduling Tips for Peer Recovery Specialists managing their own schedules

• During the first session, when peers receiving services are the most motivated, discuss the importance of regular sessions. You should also tell them about the research suggesting that having more frequent sessions in the beginning leads to longer-lasting change.

• If you have not seen your peer receiving services in a while, call them to follow-up. Best practices generally advise consistency, so develop a process with rules and stick to it. For example, if you've been seeing someone weekly, you may want to call when more than two weeks pass without an appointment.

• For ease of scheduling, offer a variety of morning, evening and weekend appointments. Also, consider implementing an on-line scheduler. The easier the scheduling process, the more likely a client is to make an appointment.

• If you go on vacation, be sure to notify your peers receiving services well in advance so they can schedule around it.

PREPARING FOR PERFORMANCE EVALUATIONS

If your company has a review process in place, mark the day on your calendar. It is recommended to ask your supervisor what established competencies are used to measure success—they can just as easily be soft skills as they can be sales targets—and then make it your business to achieve them.

Prep for Your First Performance Review

You did so well in your recent job interviews with Company X that you got the entry-level position you really wanted, but your days of having to prove your value to the company are just beginning. In a few months or perhaps even a year from now, you'll be asked to demonstrate your worth again to your supervisor during your first performance review.

Your review probably will not carry the same make-or-break pressure as your job interview. But it will still have a significant impact on your future assignments, work relationships, day-to-day activities and salary. You need to be as ready for your review, just as you were for all those interviews.

When your review is only a few weeks or days away, you must become more concrete by completing tasks like these:

Summarize Your Key Achievements

Think about and know what you achieved since you began the job and develop a written list of your most important accomplishments. Just as you might do if you were to highlight these achievements on your resume, quantify wherever possible, and mention specific results (e.g., "helped streamline the customer database, reducing request processing time by about 40 percent.").

Present These Accomplishments.

You might consider developing a career portfolio, a binder filled with items that will help you show your supervisor what you've accomplished. While you may not have the time or inclination to prepare a full-fledged portfolio featuring layout pages, divider tabs, captions for the various items and a table of contents, it is still helpful to have a nice presentation.

Develop a Detailed Agenda

If possible, have a detailed list of what you want to cover during your review meeting that is independent of your manager's agenda. That way you can also discuss what is on your mind. No matter how much you prepare, your performance review will still be at least a bit stressful. Try not to become defensive if you get some constructive criticism during the meeting and listen as much as you talk.

Check for Understanding

1. What is the difference between a vision and a goal?
2. How can you translate ideas into action?
3. What are SMART goals? What does SMART stand for?
4. What is the significance of the WDEP system?
5. How can you strengthen your own cultural awareness?

Further Application

1. Write out your own personal and professional vision statement and describe how to plan to achieve your goal.

Glossary of Terms

Accepting and Understanding: when each person is treated with unconditional positive regard is essential. Peer supporters should accept behavior as a form of communication that expresses unmet needs or emotions and help the person continue to enjoy basic personal freedoms.

Active listening: requires that the listener fully concentrate, understand, respond and then remember what is being said.

Active Reading: when you actively engage and interact with texts, rather than reading and re-reading without a clear purpose and it allows one to remain better informed.

Assertion: being direct about what you need, want, feel or believe in a way that's respectful of the views of others. It's a communication skill that can reduce conflict, build your self-confidence and improve relationships in the workplace.

Basic empathy: involves listening to people, understanding them and their concerns as best as we can, and communicating this understanding to them in such a way that they might understand themselves more fully and act on their understanding.

Career Portfolio: binder filled with items that will help you show your supervisor what you've accomplished that need not be lengthy or complicated to be effective.

Code Switching: changing the type of language used based on your audience. For example, one may use slang when talking to their friends but not with their co-workers.

Companionship: helping people in early recovery feel connected and enjoy being with others, especially in recreational activities in alcohol- and drug-free environments. This assistance is especially needed in early recovery, when little about abstaining from alcohol or drugs is reinforcing and relapse is common.

Dignity and respect: creating positive conditions where the person can live without fear of shame or ridicule; where people are treated with warmth and authenticity, listened to without judgment and are given opportunity for self-determination and self-expression.

Elevator Pitch: a succinct and persuasive sales pitch meant to be thirty to sixty seconds long.

Emotional support: demonstrations of empathy, love, caring, and concern in such activities as peer mentoring and recovery coaching, as well as recovery support groups.

Essential skills: a combination of people skills, social skills, communication skills, character traits, attitudes, career attributes, social intelligence and emotional intelligence quotients among others that enable people to navigate their environment, work well with others, perform well, and achieve their goals with complementing hard skills.

Evaluative listening: most people listen to evaluative others - his means that they are judging and labeling what the other person is saying as either right/wrong, good/bad, acceptable/unacceptable, relevant/irrelevant etc. They then tend to respond evaluatively as well.

Fact centered listening: asking only informational or factual questions won't solve the peer's problems. Listen to the peer's whole context and focus on themes and core messages.

Filtered listening: we tend to listen to ourselves, other people and the world around us through biased (often prejudiced) filters. It distorts our understanding of our peers.

Inadequate listening: people are also often distracted because they have problems of their own, feel ill, or because they become distracted by social and cultural differences between themselves and their peers. All these factors make it difficult to listen to and understand their peers.

Informational support: a provision of health and wellness information, educational assistance, and help in acquiring new skills, ranging from life skills to employment readiness and citizenship restoration.

Instrumental support: a concrete assistance in task accomplishment, especially with stressful or unpleasant tasks such as filling out applications and obtaining entitlements, providing child care, transportation to support-group meetings, and clothing closets.

Labels as filters: diagnostic labels can prevent you from really listening to your peer. If you see a peer as "that woman with Aids", your ability to listen empathetically to her problems will be severely distorted and diminished.

Numeracy: the ability to access, use, interpret and communicate mathematical information and ideas. Peers might be asked, in a daily work task, to effectively use mathematics to meet job requirements.

Person-Centered Language: imperative to mental health and substance use recovery. It must be constructive and void of blame, while using verbiage that humanizes the individual instead of identifying them by their addiction or illness

Personhood: this is a standing or status that is bestowed upon one human being by others in the context of relationship and social being. It implies recognition, respect and trust.

Probing: this involves statements and questions from the Certified Peer recovery professional that enable individuals to explore more fully any relevant issue within their lives. Probes can take the form of statements, questions, requests, single word or phrases and non-verbal prompts.

Reciprocity Principle: states that when someone does something for us, we feel obligated to return the favor.

Recognition and Individuality: knowing the individuality of each person's unique life experiences, personality, values, beliefs and opinions is a component of person-centered communication. Respect and incorporate these factors when support planning.

Rehearsing: if you mentally rehearse your answers, you are also not listening attentively. Certified Peer recovery professionals who listen carefully to the themes and core messages in a person's story always know how to respond. The response may not be a fluent, eloquent or "practiced" one, but it will at least be sincere and appropriate.

Relationships of Trust: Providing the conditions necessary to satisfy fundamental needs and create a climate for personal realization is vital. This is where the person knows confidences are respected, choice and control are maintained, and the person will not be abandoned.

Role Boundary: a clear definition of the duties, rights and limitations of facilitators, volunteers and program participants.

Scarcity: this involves letting people know that they stand to lose. In sales, it refers to attempting a quick sale by reiterating a deadline or quantity limits.

SOAP: stands for subjective, objective, assessment, and plan. The subjective portion contains a summary statement by the Peer recovery professional, which can include how the peer is feeling, along with any medical history or family history. The objective portion contains medical information that follows the subjective statement. This is usually something the Peer recovery professional completes during a peer interaction. The assessment portion contains information that the Peer recovery professional pieces together based on the interaction identifying the issue. Finally, the plan portion states the plan for future clinical work.

Social proof: the idea that people tend to follow a presented idea when they do not have sufficient information to make the decision on their own. This technique is most often used in celebrity endorsements or customer testimonials.

SWOT analysis: a tool to help you develop your professional goals and identify possible strengths and weaknesses. It stands for strengths, weaknesses, opportunities, and threats.

Sympathetic listening: It has a place in human transactions and the "use" of sympathy is limited in the helping relationship because it can distort the Certified Peer Support Worker's listening to the individual's story. To sympathize with someone is to become that person's "accomplice". Sympathy conveys pity and even complicity, and pity for the peer can diminish the extent to which you can help the person.

Works Consulted

Cheshire, S. 5 Ways to Celebrate Without Alcohol. (n.d.). Retrieved September 28, 2017, from http://www.webmd.com/mental-health/addiction/features/5-ways-to-celebrate-without-alcohol#1

DeCarlo, L. (n.d.). Answer This Job Interview Question: Tell Me (or Us) About Yourself. Retrieved September 28, 2017, from https://www.job-hunt.org/job_interviews/answering-tell-me-about-yourself-question.shtml

Erry, S. How to Get Over Your Fear of Failing at a New Job. Retrieved from https://www.themuse.com/advice/how-to-get-over-your-fear-of-failing-at-a-new-job

Falk-Ross, F. C. (2001). Toward the new literacy: Changes in college students' reading comprehension strategies following Reading/Writing projects. *Journal of Adolescent & Adult Literacy, 45*(4), 278-288.

Griffiths, G. G., Sohlberg, M. M., Kirk, C., Fickas, S., and Biancarosa, G. (2016). Evaluation of use of reading comprehension strategies to improve reading comprehension of adult college students with acquired brain injury. *Neuropsychological Rehabilitation, 26*(2), 161-190. 10.1080/09602011.2015.1007878

Lei, S. A., Rhinehart, P. J., Howard, H. A., and Cho, J. K. (2010). Strategies for improving reading comprehension among college students. *Reading Improvement, 47*(1), 30-42.

Little-Fleck, J. E. (2016, June 29). The Secret Weapon That Anyone Can Bring to an Interview to Stand Out. Retrieved September 28, 2017, from https://www.themuse.com/advice/the-secret-weapon-that-anyone-can-bring-to-an-interview-to-stand-out

Mayer, A. (n.d.). Effective Persuasion Techniques. by Alen Mayer. Retrieved from https://www.nasp.com/article/55C9EF36-96A1/effective-persuasion-techniques.html

Sack D. 5 Didn't-See-It-Coming Relapse Triggers (and How to Avoid Them). (n.d.). Retrieved September 28, 2017, from https://blogs.psychcentral.com/addiction-recovery/2012/02/addiction-relapse-triggers/

Vogt, P. Prove Yourself Again with your First Performance Review. (n.d.). Retrieved September 28, 2017, from https://www.monster.com/career-advice/article/prove-yourself-again-first-review

How to Maintain Professional Boundaries in Today's Workplace. (2017, August 11). Retrieved September 28, 2017, from https://www.roberthalf.com/blog/management-tips/how-to-maintain-professional-boundaries-in-todays-workplace

The Importance of Literacy and Numeracy Skills. (n.d.). Retrieved from https://www.kangan.edu.au/students/blog/importance-literacy-and-numeracy-skills

Department of Health & Human Services. (2012, May 31). 10 tips for being assertive. Retrieved from https://www.betterhealth.vic.gov.au/health/ten-tips/10-tips-for-being-assertive

Made in the USA
Middletown, DE
01 September 2023

37644076R00068